THE

BIBLE

A Literary Study

TWAYNE'S MASTERWORK STUDIES
Robert Lecker, General Editor

THE SCARLET LETTER: A READING
Nina Baym

MOBY-DICK: ISHMAEL'S MIGHTY BOOK
Kerry McSweeney

THE

BIBLE

A Literary Study

JOHN H. GOTTCENT

TWAYNE PUBLISHERS • BOSTON
A Division of G.K. Hall & Co.

THE BIBLE: A LITERARY STUDY
John H. Gottcent

Twayne's Masterwork Studies
No. 2

Copyright © 1986 by G.K. Hall & Co.
All Rights Reserved
Published by Twayne Publishers
A Division of G.K. Hall & Co.
70 Lincoln Street, Boston, Massachusetts 02111

Copyediting supervised by Lewis DeSimone
Designed and produced by Marne B. Sultz
Typeset in Sabon with Galliard display type
by Compset, Inc., Beverly, Massachusetts

Printed on permanent/durable acid-free paper
and bound in the United States of America

First Printing

Library of Congress Cataloging in Publication Data

Gottcent, John H.
The Bible : a literary study.

(Twayne's masterwork studies ; no. 2)
Bibliography: p. 119
1. Bible as literature.   I. Title.   II. Series.
BS535.G67   1986   809'.93522   86-9779
ISBN 0-8057-7951-5
ISBN 0-8057-8003-3 (pbk)

Once again,
to Jo

Contents

About This Book   ix
Acknowledgments   xi
The Bible: A Historical-Cultural Overview   xii
The Importance of the Bible   xxiv
Critical Reception: A Short History of the
    Literary Study of the Bible   xxviii

The Hebrew Bible (Old Testament)

    I. Reading the Bible as Literature:
       The Story of the Flood
       (*Genesis 6–9*)   3

   II. Moses: The Nature of the Hero
       (*Exodus 1–20; 32–34; Numbers 20;*
       Deuteronomy 34)   11

  III. Jephtah: The Moral Dilemma
       (*Judges 11*)   18

  IV. Samson: Another Slant on the Hero
       (*Judges 13–16*)   26

   V. Saul: A Tragic Hero?
       (*1 Samuel 8–31*)   31

  VI. David: A Study in Politics
       (*1 Samuel 16–31; 2 Samuel 1–24;*
       1 Kings 1:1–2:12)   38

 VII. Elijah and Ahab: Another Portrait of Divinity
       (*1 Kings 17–22; 2 Kings 1–2*)   47

VIII. Jonah: Two Problems with Thinking
       (*Jonah 1–4*)   55

  IX. Psalm 23: The Maturing of Faith   60

X. Job: The Problem of Suffering
(*Job 1–42*)   66

XI. Ruth: A Study in Interpersonal Relationships
(*Ruth 1–4*)   74

XII. Ecclesiastes: Disillusionment and
Our Philosophical Personality
(*Ecclesiastes 1–12*)   82

The New Testament

XIII. The Good Samaritan: A Question of Ethics
(*Luke 10:25–37*)   91

XIV. The Prodigal Son: Family Jealousies and Justice
(*Luke 15:11–32*)   96

XV. Acts of the Apostles:
The Archetypal Birthing Process
(*Acts 1–15*)   101

XVI. Revelation: "The Sense of an Ending"
(*Revelation 1–22*)   109

Epilogue: Some Conclusions   116
Selected Bibliography   119
Index   124
About the Author   126

About This Book

This is a study of the most famous piece of writing in the Western world. It takes an unusual perspective, however, approaching the Bible not as theology, not as history, but as literature. To some extent, it places the Bible in the context of world literature.

In an age of literary "schools" ranging from New Criticism to deconstruction, reading the Bible "as literature" can mean many things. I've tried to explain my own, eclectic methodology in chapter 1. But for now, let me say that—like most literary people—I try to acknowledge the religious dimension of the Bible but steer clear of advocating doctrinal positions; similarly, I accept the source and redaction theories of most modern scholarship, but prefer to work with the final text. Naturally, only a few selections from biblical material can be treated in a volume of this size, but I hope enough is here to illustrate the exciting possibilities of literary study and to whet your appetite for more.

Throughout this book, I've preferred the term *literary analysis* to the more familiar *literary criticism*. The latter is confusing because it is used in different senses by biblical scholars—for whom it usually means source study—and by literary people—for whom it means interpretation. I find *literary analysis* a more neutral term, but if I do occasionally resort to *literary criticism*—for stylistic reasons, or when quoting—it will always mean interpretation.

Several other terms need explanation. You will notice I prefer to call the first section of biblical material treated here the "Hebrew Bible" or "Hebrew Scriptures" instead of "Old Testament." The latter term, while undoubtedly more familiar to most readers, creates problems. For one thing, Christians don't always agree on what constitutes the Old Testament; in most Protestant Bibles, for example, it consists of thirty-nine books, while in Roman Catholic versions it contains forty-six, some of which include material not found in their Protestant counterparts. More important, the negative connotations of "old" are bothersome to many Jewish readers for whom this material is not in the least out of date. Since our approach is nonsectarian, I will confine myself to material in this part of the Bible common to all major traditions, and for the most part avoid "Old Testament." The terms "Hebrew Bible" or "Hebrew Scriptures" have the added advantage of reminding us that this material is not only a religious document, but a cultural record of a people, written (except for a few passages) in the Hebrew language. For similar reasons, I will approach the books of the Hebrew Bible in their traditional order of Torah-Prophets-Writings (see "The Bible: A Historical-Cultural Overview" for more details), rather than the Law-History-Poetry-Prophecy arrangement found in most Christian Bibles. But you can read these chapters, of course, in any order, depending on your preferred approach.

In a similar vein, I will avoid the initials B.C. and A.D. in reference to dates and substitute B.C.E. (which can be understood as either "Before the Christian Era" or "Before the Common Era") and C.E. ("Christian/Common Era"). Now widely used by scholars, these labels have the same significance as their traditional counterparts; thus the year 586 B.C.E. is the same as 586 B.C., and 33 C.E. the same as 33 A.D.

Two other terms that might cause confusion are *the Lord* and *Yahweh*. The latter is, in effect, the personal name of the Israelite God (as Zeus is the name of a Greek god). It is related to the Hebrew verb *to be*, but is never translated and, out of respect, seldom printed in modern versions, which usually substitute *the Lord*. I will prefer *the Lord*, but occasionally—especially to stress the personal identity of this divinity—will use *Yahweh*. For most intents and purposes, the labels are interchangeable.

I have worked throughout with the Revised Standard Version of the Bible, a translation that preserves much of the flavor of the King James while greatly improving its accuracy. All quotations, unless otherwise noted, are from that Bible, though all underscoring within quotations is mine. You can work without difficulty with any modern translation, however; some standard ones are listed in the bibliography at the end of this volume.

Biblical citations follow conventional format; thus Exo. 3:14 means the Book of Exodus, chapter 3, verse 14, and 1 Kings 19:4–20:6 means a passage of the First Book of Kings beginning at chapter 19, verse 4, and ending at chapter 20, verse 6. The letters *a* or *b* refer, respectively, to the first or second half of a verse; thus Luke 10:25b identifies the latter part of that verse.

A final note about the interpretive readings that make up the bulk of this study. They are meant not as definitive critical essays, but as illustrations of, and invitations to, literary analysis of the Bible. Though I hope they contain useful insights, don't feel, having read any one of them, that you have the complete and final word on that biblical material. These are not *the* readings of the text—I don't think such absolute interpretations exist—but *my* readings. To emphasize this, I've made frequent use of the first person singular throughout my comments. But you should always feel free to add to, detract from, or challenge my conclusions. Only in this way can I fulfill my purpose of helping make each reader a literary analyst of his or her own.

Acknowledgments

All biblical material is taken from the Revised Standard Version of the Bible, copyright 1946, 1952, © 1971, 1973, and quoted by permission.

The section "Critical Reception: A Short History of the Literary Study of the Bible" is expanded and updated from the introduction to my book *The Bible as Literature: A Selective Bibliography* (Boston: G.K. Hall & Co., 1979). Some of the annotations in the bibliography are adapted from the same source.

The frontispiece is reproduced through the kind permission of Penn Prints of New York.

I also want to thank a number of individuals who have helped with the project in various ways, especially Ronald Gottesman, Herbert Marks, Steven Scheer, and Thayer Warshaw. My division chairman, James R. Blevins, has given much encouragement and support. Robert Lecker and the staff at Twayne Publishers have been most helpful. And as always, my wife, JoAnne, has provided invaluable assistance, especially during typing and editing. Naturally, none of these people is responsible for any weaknesses in the finished product.

The Bible: A Historical-Cultural Overview

To Christians the Bible consists of two sections: the Old and New Testaments. To Jews it is composed only of the Hebrew Scriptures, roughly equivalent to the Protestant Old Testament. (In the Roman Catholic and some other Christian traditions there are additional books in the Old Testament, considered authoritative by neither Jews nor most Protestants.) In this survey I want to consider the two Christian sections separately, beginning with the Old Testament (which I'll call the Hebrew Bible) and proceeding to the New.

What Is the Hebrew Bible?

The Hebrew Bible–identical in substance, but not in order and arrangement, to the Protestant Old Testament—constitutes a record, composed over many centuries, of the Jewish people's view of God's contractual agreement with them. (The word *testament* means "agreement" or "covenant.") It is traditionally divided into three sections, each of which came to be *canonized*—that is, officially declared sacred writing—at a different time.

The first, and most sacred, section is the *Torah* (Hebrew for "instruction" or "law"); an alternate term often applied to the same material is *Pentateuch* (Greek for "five scrolls"). Here we find the books of Genesis, Exodus, Leviticus, Numbers, and Deuteronomy, with their accounts of the origin of the universe, the earliest history of the Jewish people, and their code of laws. The canonization of the Torah was probably completed in the fifth century B.C.E. (Before the Christian/Common Era). Although the material is traditionally ascribed to Moses, modern scholars believe it was collected, edited, and reworked by a number of writers over many centuries.

The second major division of the Hebrew Scriptures is the *Prophets;* it is usually subdivided into *Former* and *Latter Prophets.* (The term *Prophets* here refers to books, not people, and *Former* and *Latter* to position in the text, not chronology.) The Former Prophets consist of Joshua, Judges, and the two books each of Samuel and Kings. They don't contain much "prophecy" in the modern sense; instead they continue the history of the Israelites through the end of the sixth century B.C.E. The Latter Prophets include Isaiah, Jeremiah, Ezekiel, and the Minor Prophets (originally one long book, now usually printed as twelve shorter ones); these are the books commonly thought of as "prophetic" today. The canonization of the Prophets was probably completed in the third century B.C.E.

The final division is the *Writings* (or Sacred Writings or Hagiographa, which is Greek for the same thing). This is a kind of grab-bag category containing everything not in the Torah or Prophets: Psalms, Job, Proverbs, Ruth, Song of Songs, Ecclesiastes, Lamentations, Esther, Daniel, Ezra-Nehemiah, and Chronicles. Considered least sacred for religious purposes (books like Song of Songs and Ecclesiastes were accepted only after great debate among the rabbis), this category contains some of the best literature in the Hebrew Bible. Though some of these books gained authoritative stature earlier, the Writings as a whole were not canonized until around 90 C.E. (Christian/Common Era), when the canon was closed; thus the "Old Testament" as known today was not fixed until more than half a century *after* the death of Jesus.

The division into Torah-Prophets-Writings is still followed in modern Jewish Bibles but not in Christian ones, as a glance at the table of contents of many recent translations will quickly show. (Christian Bibles arrange their Old Testaments into books of Law, History, Poetry, and Prophecy.) In our study, I will approach the books in their traditional Hebrew order.

Historical Background:
The Era of the Hebrew Scriptures

Though we are not studying the Bible as history, some knowledge of historical background is helpful, and sometimes essential, for an understanding of the text. In this section I will briefly summarize some major events in the history of ancient Israel and offer three observations about that history.

As is the case with all cultures, the history of Israel is dotted with major events and eras that left a permanent mark on the people's culture and consciousness. Of these, the following ten are particularly important:

1. *The Age of the Patriarchs* (ca. 1800–1500 [unless otherwise indicated, throughout this section, all dates should be understood as B.C.E.]). Abraham was a nomadic Mesopotamian called by the Lord to become the father of the Jewish people. (His name in Hebrew suggests "father of a multitude.") Throughout the centuries they saw in him and in his grandson Jacob (later renamed "Israel") both the progenitors and symbols of their race. Even in New Testament times a Jew identified himself as "a descendant of Abraham."

2. *Israel in Egypt* (ca. 1500–1240). The descendants of Abraham migrated to Egypt (a phenomenon given biblical explanation in the story of Joseph in Gen. 37–50) and were eventually enslaved by the Egyptians and put to work building cities for Pharaoh— the first of many times that Israel would come under foreign domination.

3. *The Exodus* (ca. 1240–1200). Led by Moses, the Israelites escaped from Egypt and migrated across the Sinai toward Palestine. This is the central event in ancient Israel's history, always looked back to by later generations as that time in which God most clearly showed his special relationship to this people. Celebrated annually in the feast of Passover, it is to the Jew what the Resurrection of Jesus is to the Christian. In another sense, the Exodus was to Israel what the Revolutionary War was to the

United States: the great unifying event that gave its people the common bond of a struggle for freedom.

4. *The Period of the Judges* (ca. 1200–1020). The Israelites settled into Palestine over a number of decades and eventually established a Tribal League: a loose confederation of tribes bound together by a common religion but lacking a central government. Leadership came into the hands of judges like Deborah, Jephtah, and Samson, who arose to meet crises as they developed.

5. *The Monarchy* (ca. 1020–922). The Israelites argued intensely over the issue of monarchy, some seeing the need for a human leader and others maintaining there should be no king but the Lord. Eventually the former won out, and Saul was anointed first king of Israel. His reign was chaotic, but his successor, David, established a great kingdom that became the high-water mark of Israelite political power, one of the few times when Israel was an independent and significant state in the Near East. David's reign was later looked upon as the time of greatest glory for Israel, and the tradition developed that a Messiah would come from his royal line. But David's son, Solomon, builder of the magnificent Temple, proved the last ruler of a short-lived united kingdom.

6. *The Divided Kingdom* (922–722). After Solomon's death the kingdom was divided, the northern section retaining the name Israel and eventually establishing its capital at Samaria, while the smaller southern section, now called Judah, maintained its capital at Jerusalem. The great age of the prophets began as figures like Elijah in the north and Isaiah in the south fought to keep the people faithful to the Lord in the face of competing cultures and religions.

7. *The Destruction of Israel and the Survival of Judah* (722–587). By the second half of the eighth century the Assyrian Empire had become a dominant and oppressive force in the Near East, threatening the independence of neighboring states. In 722, Sargon II destroyed the northern kingdom, and Israel would never again exist as a political entity in biblical times. Thousands of Israelites were deported to the east, and Gentiles (non-Jews) were brought in to intermarry with those who remained. (These were the ancestors of the Samaritans.) The southern kingdom, though threat-

ened, survived, and biblical history became the story of Judah.

8. *The Babylonian Exile* (587–538). Though it survived the Assyrian threat, Judah itself eventually fell to the Babylonians, who in 587 tore down the Temple, destroyed Jerusalem, and carted thousands of Jews to Babylon. The resulting Exile—also called the Captivity or the Deportation—was the low point in the history of Judah and seemed to spell the end of the Jewish nation. But in 538, the Persian leader Cyrus, conqueror of Babylonia, granted freedom to the exiled Jews, many of whom trekked back toward Jerusalem to rebuild the city and the Temple.

9. *Diaspora and Restoration* (538–167). Following the Edict of Cyrus, many Jews did not return to Palestine but took up residence in other cities, beginning a phenomenon called the *Diaspora* (Greek for "dispersion"); previously, being a Jew had meant following a certain religion *and* living in a certain country, but now it meant only the former. These people began to absorb both the culture and the language of their new residences. Meanwhile, in Palestine, restoration of the community began under the leadership of Nehemiah and Ezra. But even here a return to the status quo was not possible: the Second Temple never rivaled the magnificence of the First, and slowly but surely, Hebrew was lost as an everyday language, replaced by Aramaic. Most important, restored Jews were not politically independent: Cyrus allowed exiles to return home, but Palestine remained under Persian control. In later centuries it would pass into the hands of the Greeks (under Alexander the Great), the Ptolemies (an Egyptian dynasty), and the Seleucids (a Syrian power).

10. *The Maccabean Era* (167–63). Conditions under the Persians, Greeks, and Ptolemies were at least tolerable, but the Seleucids proved insufferably oppressive, taxing the people heavily and defiling the Temple by erecting within it a statue of Zeus. In the mid–second century, a Jewish revolt was led by the Maccabee family; when it proved successful, the country was again ruled by its own people, descendants of the Maccabees. The revolt was the one bright spot in the last five centuries of Jewish scriptural history. A symbol of determination and perseverance under the most trying circumstances, it is celebrated annually in the feast of Cha-

nukah. The century of relative independence it ushered in ended only with the Romans, whose annexation of Palestine brings us into the New Testament period.

This sketchy outline only begins to scratch the surface, but it does lead to three important observations about the history of ancient Israel. The first is this: since that history really begins with Abraham, the Bible's opening narratives—the stories of Creation, Eden, Cain and Abel, Noah, and Babel—represent a kind of preface to what follows. The heroes of those stories are not seen as Jews but as progenitors of all humankind, and their narratives should be read as a sort of mythic prehistory.

Second, the Jews spent the early part of their scriptural period as nomadic wanderers, not becoming a nation in the modern sense until nearly the time of David. They were a migratory people who traveled from Mesopotamia to Canaan to Egypt, back to Canaan, back to Egypt, and back again to Canaan. They lived in tents and tended flocks. A small, apparently tightly-knit band, they had no land of their own until the time of the Judges, no central government until the monarchy. The first books of the Hebrew Bible must be read against this nomadic background.

The third, and most important, observation is this: throughout their entire history, the Jews were a people almost constantly dominated by foreign powers. It began with the Egyptians in the centuries prior to the Exodus and continued as almost every empire that came to power in the Near East impinged on or controlled Israel: the Assyrians, the Babylonians, the Persians, the Greeks, the Ptolemies, the Seleucids, and eventually, the Romans. Jewish autonomy was rare.

This forced mingling with other peoples inevitably left its mark on Jewish culture. Sometimes the effects were destructive: the Assyrians permanently annihilated northern Israel, and the Babylonian Exile led to a disunifying Diaspora. In other ways, they were positive: the Egyptian enslavement helped mold Israel into a unified whole, and the Exile (which nearly spelled the end of Judaism) inspired the Jews to leave a permanent written record of their traditions, resulting in the Bible. Yet through it all, the people endured, as they do today. Historians have observed that no culture has survived in recognizable form as long as

Jewish culture. In many ways, the Scriptures are a record of the earliest stages of this endurance.

What is the New Testament?

The New Testament is the name assigned by Christians to their canonized collection of writings centering around the life and teachings of Jesus and the early Church. It emphasizes the Christian view of a new agreement between God and his people, something hinted at in the Hebrew Bible but now brought into sharper focus. (In a famous maxim, Augustine wrote, "The New Testament is concealed in the Old, the Old Testament revealed in the New.") About one-third the length of the Hebrew Bible, it also covers a much shorter time span: approximately 100 years (ca. 6 B.C.E. – ca. 95 C.E.) as opposed to at least 1500 years.

The twenty-seven books of the New Testament are sometimes divided into four categories, though these are less strictly defined than the Torah, Prophets, and Writings of the Hebrew Bible. First come the *Gospels:* four accounts of the life, teachings, death, and Resurrection of Jesus. The first three—those of Matthew, Mark, and Luke—are often called the *Synoptic Gospels* because there are many parallels among them (*synoptic* derives from a Greek word suggesting "a viewing together"). In contrast, the fourth Gospel—that of John—has less in common with the other three; its tone is different, and it includes several incidents (among them Jesus' conversations with Nicodemus and the raising of Lazarus) not reported elsewhere.

The second category, *Church History,* contains but one book: the Acts of the Apostles. This is actually a continuation of Luke's Gospel, tracing the early struggles of the Christian community and introducing the apostle Paul.

Third we find the *Letters:* pieces of correspondence addressed to Christian communities or individuals by apostolic writers. There are far more books here—twenty-one—than in any other division of the New Testament, and they are sometimes subdivided into the thirteen Letters ascribed to Paul, the unsigned Letter to the Hebrews (occasionally called Pauline but from ancient times considered anonymous), and the seven catholic ("universal") Letters—two of Peter, three of

John, one each of James and Jude—so called because by and large they are not addressed to a particular audience.

Finally, the New Testament ends with a book of *Apocalyptic:* the Revelation of John. Reminiscent of the second half of Daniel, this book depicts a series of visions of the end of the world and thus provides a fitting conclusion to the Christian Bible.

Historical Background:
The Era of the New Testament

The following survey touches on only a few highlights of the period from mid–first century B.C.E. to mid–second century C.E.

1. *The Maccabean Era* (ca. 167–63 B.C.E.). We have seen how in post-Exilic times Palestine was ruled by a succession of empires—Persian, Greek, Ptolemaic, and Seleucid—and how a successful revolt led by the Maccabee family broke the Seleucid stronghold and introduced a semblance of independence. In fact, descendants of the Maccabees, called Hasmoneans, ruled Israel as kings. Though popular among some, the Hasmoneans came to be known for ruthless practices that led other Jews to long for a new "anointed one" (Messiah) to be raised up by God.

2. *The Intervention of Rome* (63–37 B.C.E.). In the year 63 an internal power struggle led several Jewish groups to appeal for help to Rome, by now firmly entrenched as a world power. The Roman general Pompey entered Jerusalem himself and settled the dispute by force; unfortunately, his troops did not leave. Palestine was annexed to the Roman province of Syria, and a weak Hasmonean, John Hyrcanus II, was named not king, but high priest. Real power shifted into the hands of an Idumean named Antipater, technically an advisor to Hyrcanus but actually the representative of Rome. And so the Romans took their place beside the other empirical powers who had held sway in Palestine.

3. *The Age of Herod the Great* (37–4 B.C.E.). In the year 37, the Roman leader Octavian (later known as Caesar Augustus) appointed Antipater's son Herod (called "the Great" to distinguish him from other Herods in the New Testament) as new king of Israel. Follow-

ing a typical Roman arrangement, Herod ruled with considerable local authority, though ultimate power was retained by Rome. (The circumstances were not unlike those that prevail in the twentieth century between the Soviet Union and its satellite countries.) He was generally hated by the Jews for at least three reasons: his devotion to Rome, his questionable ancestry (the Idumeans had been conquered and forcibly converted to Judaism by an earlier Jewish king; thus Herod was considered only a "half-Jew"), and his vindictive, unstable behavior (Matthew's account of Herod's order that all Bethlehem infants be killed to eliminate Jesus as a possible threat to the throne is consistent with other reports of the king's manner). Still, he held a firm grip on the country and began a massive building program that included a reconstruction of the dilapidated Temple. Jesus was born during his reign, in about 6 B.C.E. (The strange date results from the miscalculation of the medieval monk—appropriately named Dennis the Short—who computed the Christian calendar.)

4. *The Post-Herodian Age* (4 B.C.E.–37 C.E.). Upon Herod's death his kingdom was divided among three of his sons. The northeastern portion, including Iturea and Trachonitis, went to Philip. (It was he who married Herodias, a woman later claimed by his brother in an act denounced by John the Baptist; see Mark 6:17–18.) The districts of Galilee and Perea went to Herod Antipas. (Jesus, as a Galilean resident of Nazareth, grew up under his jurisdiction. This is also the Herod before whom Jesus appeared as part of his trial; see Luke 23:6–12.) The central district of Judea—including Jerusalem and hence the prize plum in the package—went to a third son, Archelaus. But he proved such a bad ruler that the Romans sent him packing in 6 C.E. and assigned the administration of Judea to a Roman procurator, or governor. (Pontius Pilate, instrumental in the Passion narratives, was procurator of Judea from 26–36 C.E.) To be sure, the procurator was assisted in local government by the Great Sanhedrin, a judicial council of some seventy Jews presided over by the high priest. (It was the Sanhedrin before whom Jesus first appeared on the night of his trial; see Matthew 26:57–68.) This council notwithstanding, the notion that the holy city was now directly ruled by a foreign power was infuriating to

many Jews, but the situation was to prevail throughout the lifetime of Jesus.

5. *Palestine after Jesus* (37–66 C.E.). Jesus was probably crucified in 27 C.E. Beginning about ten years later, local authority in Palestine began to pass into the hands of Herod the Great's grandson, Herod Agrippa I, who ruled as king, eventually extending his domain to essentially the same territory controlled by his grandfather. Upon Agrippa's death in 44, Judea was once again administered by pro-curators, two of whom—Felix and Festus—appear in the Book of Acts in connection with Paul.

6. *The First Jewish Revolt* (66–73 C.E.). Jewish unrest under Roman rule reached a crisis point in 66 when a group of radicals seized control of the government and declared independence from Rome. Thus began the Jewish Wars; an important account of them by the Jewish but pro-Roman historian Josephus survives to this day. The Romans eventually overpowered the Jews, recapturing Jerusalem in 70 and virtually destroying the city as the Babylonians had done centuries before; the Temple was never rebuilt. By 73 all Jewish resistance, including that at the famous outpost of Massada, had been overcome. But the fires of revolt were not yet extinguished.

7. *Temporary Calm and the Revolt of Bar-Kochbah* (73-135 C.E.). An uneasy peace, interrupted by scattered uprisings, saw Palestine through a succession of Roman emperors for sixty years. But in 132 a powerful Jewish leader, Simon Bar-Kochbah ("son of a star") instigated a second revolt. For a while it was successful, with Bar-Kochbah hailed by some as the Messiah. But in 135 Rome again prevailed, and the ancient state of Israel came to an end. The emperor Hadrian forbade any Jew from entering Jerusalem and erected a temple to Jupiter therein. Judaism as a religion continued, its center moving to Babylonia, but Israel as a distinct nation would not reemerge until the twentieth century.

Judaism in the First Century

Although Christianity would later be dominated by Gentiles, its founder and earliest practitioners were decidedly Jewish. And a common misconception is that the Judaism they were part of was a monolithic phenomenon. While most Jews shared some common beliefs (for example, respect for the Torah as divine revelation), their religion was divided along sectarian lines (much like modern Christianity), and it will help us to know a little about the major Jewish "denominations" of the time.

1. *The Sadducees.* These conservative aristocrats were the most influential Jews in Jesus' lifetime. They relied for their doctrine only on the written Torah of Moses, rejecting all other biblical books (remember that the canon of the Hebrew Bible was not firmly set in Jesus' day) and the teachings unique to them, including belief in resurrection and the imminence of a Messiah. The debate between Jesus and the Sadducees (see Mark 12:18–27) reflects their skepticism about resurrection, a notion generally accepted at this time by other Jews.

2. *The Pharisees.* This is the sect receiving most notice in the New Testament, almost all of it bad (probably for reasons I will note in a moment). They accepted not only the Torah, but also the "newer" Prophets and Writings; in fact, the Pharisees established the final canon of the Hebrew Bible near the end of the first century C.E. They also adhered to a system of oral tradition through which they continually tried to adapt the Mosaic law to everyday situations. Extremists among them are attacked in the Gospels for excessive pedantry, but on the whole the Pharisees were probably trying to take their religion seriously as a part of everyday life. After the fall of Jerusalem in 70, they became the most prominent sect, essentially defining normative Judaism. The fact that the Gospels were composed around this time, while Christianity was beginning to distinguish itself from Judaism, may explain the bad press the Pharisees receive in the New Testament and later Christian tradition.

3. *The Zealots.* These were radicals advocating the overthrow of Roman rule. They instigated a number of uprisings, culminating in the ultimately disastrous Jewish Wars of 66–73 C.E. At least one of Jesus' immediate followers, called Simon the Zealot (see Luke 6:15), was associated with the group. An older tradition claimed that Judas Iscariot, the betrayer of Jesus, was a Zealot, but there is little evidence to support the contention.

4. *The Essenes.* This small pious sect has received considerable attention in the twentieth century following the discovery of the Dead Sea Scrolls, which they produced. They lived in the wilderness, in an isolated communal society of celibates, deliberately separating themselves from the Jerusalem Jews they considered "polluted." They spent much time studying Scripture and preserving their purity, anxiously awaiting that moment when God would intervene in history in a dramatic battle between the "sons of light" and the "sons of darkness." An older tradition claimed John the Baptist might have been an Essene, but more recent scholarship suggests these separatists had little direct impact on first-century Jews or Christians.

In a very real sense, Christianity began as another of these subcultures within Judaism. The earliest Christians were called Nazarenes (that is, followers of the one from Nazareth); they remained pious Jews, as accounts in the early chapters of Acts suggest. Indeed, the whole notion of admitting Gentiles into Christianity proved a divisive issue that rocked the early Church. Only toward the end of the first century, as the Greek followers of Paul began to dominate, did the break between Christianity and Judaism become complete.

The Composition, Collection, and Canonization of the New Testament

Virtually all the books of the New Testament were written in the Greek language during the second half of the first century C.E. Order of composition, however, is not reflected in present biblical order; indeed, all of Paul's Letters probably predate the Gospels, though they are always printed following them. Besides the twenty-seven books eventually canonized, a number of other Christian works emerged, receiving more or less respect in different communities. (By one account, at least thirty gospels were in existence at the end of the fifth century.) The prologue to Luke (1:1–4) seems to refer to part of this group, some of which survives to this day as the New Testament Apocrypha.

At first, the books were preserved and circulated as a means of communication among early Christian communities. The first to be collected were likely some of the Pauline Letters. Later, Gospels—especially Luke—were added; this early collection was often divided into "Gospel" and "Apostle."

The process of canonization itself was slow. The earliest Christians seem to have considered only the Jewish Bible (most likely in the Greek translation called the Septuagint) as Scripture. But gradually, respect grew for Christian writings as divine revelation. Some books were accepted readily, while others—among them James, Jude, 2 Peter, 2 and 3 John, and Revelation—were subjects of debate. The issue was not resolved for several centuries, the "official" acceptance of the present twenty-seven books being usually linked to Bishop Athanasius of Alexandria, who in the year 367 wrote an important letter identifying them as the New Testament. His list was followed by Jerome in the Vulgate, an important Latin translation of the Bible. The present order of the books was suggested by Augustine in 397. After the fourth century, the canon went virtually unchallenged.

It is as a combination of Hebrew Scriptures and New Testament that the Bible has had its most profound impact on Western civilization. In the next section, we will consider why it remains an important object of study today.

The Importance of the Bible

Given the incredible number of biblical studies produced each year, one might justifiably ask, do we really need another? Put another way, why does the Bible matter, especially in a secular context, and why do we continue to read and study it? I want to suggest five answers, moving from the more to the less obvious, from the tangentially significant (in terms of the present study) to the centrally important, and to conclude with a series of reasons that the Bible should particularly be read as literature.

The most obvious answer to why the Bible matters is its religious significance: it is a sacred text for Judaism, Christianity, and (indirectly, in that it is viewed by Muslims as authentic revelation for its time) Islam. For many it is the only book of real importance, the answer to the central problems of life, the Word of God. And this makes it cru-cial—not just for the believer, but also for the non-believer, who must understand the faithful with whom he lives, and who can find in the Bible a source of the believer's doctrine (for example, the concept of resurrection), ritual (the Jewish Passover and Christian Eucharist are both modeled on biblical practices), and ethics (debates on issues like capital punishment and nuclear warfare often cite the Bible—on all sides of the question). Regarding this last, the notion that one can "prove anything" by quoting the Bible does not reduce the book to a worthless hodgepodge of self-contradictions (many arguers select their favorite verses out of context), but makes it an essential tool for un-derstanding various positions.

A second reason for the Bible's importance is its unparalleled influ-ence on language and the arts. Especially through the King James Ver-sion, the Bible helped shape the English language; whole phrases ("the apple of his eye," "the skin of my teeth," "the salt of the earth," "a thorn in the flesh") have worked their way into everyday, non-reli-gious conversation. It is the source of innumerable literary allusions (in believing writers like Dante and Shakespeare, and skeptics like Vol-taire and Vonnegut) and the subject matter of art (Da Vinci's *Last Supper*, Michaelangelo's Sistine Chapel) and of music (Handel's *Mes-siah*). In short, one can hardly speak, read, or respond to the fine arts without encountering the Bible.

Still, important as its religious and linguistic/artistic significance is, these factors are only indirectly related to our present study. An issue closer to home is this third argument: the Bible matters because it is at the foundation of Western culture. As a primary source of historical information about such things as the Exodus, the kingdom of David, the early Church, it puts us in touch with our roots, with our cultural heritage, and answers questions such as: what were these ancient peo-ple like? what were their values, and how did they help shape ours? On another level, literary specialist Northrop Frye has repeatedly ar-gued that the Bible is the central myth of Western culture, the ency-clopedic form that constitutes "the great code" of literature; he sees in its (for him) single unified narrative from creation to apocalypse a pattern that underlies the imaginative tradition of our world. And this cultural significance is not just a vestige from the remote past. The Bible continues to play a major role in shaping American society. Even in the 1980s a secular magazine like *Newsweek* can conclude "that the Bible, perhaps even more than the Constitution, is our founding document: the source of the powerful myth of the United States as a special, sacred nation, a people called by God to establish a model society, a beacon to the world."

Fourth, the Bible needs to be studied because of the great amount of ignorance surrounding it. Ironically, it may be the most revered, yet least read, book in the world. Gallup polls have shown that while the majority of Americans believe the Bible divinely inspired, fewer than half can name even four of the Ten Commandments. In the academic world, though the Bible is on virtually everyone's "required reading" list, the basic facts it states are not well known. Diagnostic quizzes I've given college students repeatedly reveal popular misconceptions: that the Genesis serpent is explicitly identified as Satan, that Eve is tempted with an apple, that Samson is married to Delilah, Jonah swallowed by a whale, Jesus visited by three wise men. (Such notions usually add a certainty to what the text leaves ambiguous; Matthew, for example, does not specify the number of wise men.) Perhaps the most damaging misconception about the Bible, however, is the prejudicial belief that its characters are all straitlaced, tedious saints whose stories demonstrate a steadfast—and boring—piety. I've found students amazed, and exhilarated, by the sight of Saul—chosen by the Lord—hiding among the baggage when the time has come to acclaim him king; by David—greatest of the Israelite monarchs—scheming to arrange the death of his soldier in order to take his wife; by the writer of Ecclesiastes, admitting with soul-searching honesty that the good are not always rewarded, the bad not always punished; by the depiction of the Lord as a God who can create humanity and then wish he hadn't, who can attempt to kill Moses for no apparent reason, who can deliberately place a lying spirit in the mouths of his prophets. Contrary to widespread opinion, the Bible is filled with reading that surprises and fascinates.

I have saved for last the argument that for me is most important: the Bible is significant because, as with all great literature, reading it is a source of insight into human experience. Hans-Georg Gadamer defined a classic as "that which speaks in such a way that it is not a statement about what is past, a mere testimony to something that still needs to be interpreted, but says something to the present as if it were said specifically to it." That the Bible meets this criterion can be seen by looking at the kinds of questions our study will raise: what is a hero? how do we resolve a moral dilemma? what marks the rise and fall of political careers? why do the innocent suffer? what character-izes and motivates interpersonal relationships? I will try to show that such questions are of vital concern to us in the late twentieth century. And so are other questions, about the nature of faith or of divinity itself—not because they are "religious" questions, but because they are human questions at the core of our lives. Reading the Bible can help us think about these issues, illuminate our experience, identify and refine our opinions.

There are many reasons, then, that the Bible matters. But for us there remains an additional concern: why subject it to *literary* analy-sis? What does this perspective provide that more traditional theolog-ical or scholarly approaches often do not? I think there are at least four answers.

First, literary analysis of the Bible reminds us that much of its text appears in the form of literature, either as narrative with plot, char-acters, dialogue, action, and an implicit theme, or verse with such tra-ditional features as metaphor, repetition, rhythm, parallelism, and imagery. Second, as the issues raised a moment ago suggest, such anal-ysis can provide useful information about human experience—expe-rience that includes, but is not limited to, what we usually mean by "religion." (This says to me that traditional definitions are too narrow, that political careers and interpersonal relationships may be inextric-ably bound up with religious experience too.)

Third, literary study provides a way of taking the Bible to heart. Many readers, no matter what their religious perspective, are so awed by the Bible's reputation that they are afraid to touch it, either for fear of sacrilege or for fear they will be "seduced" into believing it. Literary study invites us to wrestle with the text, to analyze the experience of reading it, and to grow from the process. Finally, a literary approach provides an appropriate means of interpreting the Bible. Given the ancient world's basically mythic perspective, literature was a natural mode of expression for biblical writers, more appropriate for conveying the highest truths than the discursive analysis that would dominate later ages. We may carefully separate history from literature, "fact" from "fiction," but many ancient writers blurred the distinction. For them, story meant truth, on several levels. Literary study is thus a valid method of responding to their texts.

The Bible remains an enduring legacy, influencing not only our religion, but our entire world. Reading it as literature should provide an intriguing and useful perspective on its significance for our time.

Critical Reception: A Short History of the Literary Study of the Bible

Though C. S. Lewis claimed our age invented the phrase "Bible as literature," interest in this approach can be traced far back into history—perhaps to the Bible itself. An early literary method, allegorical interpretation, was used by Jesus to explain one of his parables (Matt. 13:18–23), and Paul often read the Hebrew Scriptures the same way; in Galatians, for example, he interpreted Abraham's two sons as allegorical references to covenants applying to his own day—without, by the way, denying the historicity of Abraham's family (4:21–31). Paul's important distinction between the "written code" (traditionally, "letter") that kills and the "Spirit" that gives life (2 Cor. 3:6) became, under the influence of Origen and Augustine, the basic justification for much medieval allegorizing of Scripture; such readings assumed a hidden meaning ("spirit") imbedded in the written word.

The earliest extrabiblical example of a literary comment on the Bible may be a single sentence in *On the Sublime*, a first-century C.E. treatise on style long attributed to Longinus; in the midst of its discussion of powerful descriptions of divinities in classical literature we suddenly find: "So too the lawgiver of the Jews, no ordinary person, having formed a high conception of the power of the Divine Being, gave expression to it when at the very beginning of his Laws he wrote:

'God said'—what? 'Let there be light, and there was light; let there be land, and there was land.'" Longinus's influence blossomed in the Renaissance, when attention was paid to the style and power of biblical literature. Sir Philip Sidney's *Defense of Poesy* (1583) included an argument that the Psalms and parables of the Bible be seen as powerful literature, and John Milton's "Reason of Church Government" (1642), in comparing its author and his mission to the ancient Hebrew writers, justified parts of the Bible as literature.

It was the eighteenth century, however, that produced the first significant and extended literary analyses of the Bible. The pioneering study was the work of Bishop Robert Lowth, whose *Lectures on the Sacred Poetry of the Hebrews* examined many facets of biblical poetry and is usually credited with first noting the characteristic Hebrew use of poetic parallelism as a principle of versification. (Earlier writers had questioned the apparent absence of familiar metrical forms in the Bible; Lowth argued that parallelism—in simple terms, a close grammatical or semantic correspondence between two halves of a verse—was the basis for such work.) In Germany, Johann Gottfried von Herder's *The Spirit of Hebrew Poetry* defended the Bible as literature and presented specific studies of selected biblical poems; Herder's work heralded the romantic criticism of the next century.

This romantic fascination with biblical literature echoed through the nineteenth century in isolated praises of the power, style, and beauty of biblical verses. Walt Whitman's comment epitomizes the attitude: "Even to our Nineteenth Century here are the fountain heads of song." Concurrently, this century saw the rise of "Higher Criticism"; its concern for authorship and history paved the way for the major interests of biblical scholars in our era who, in contrast to most literary analysts, dissect the text into antecedents and sources. But at least one writer has argued that even the earlier higher critics took a more holistic approach and, in their concern for myth, treated much of the Bible as literature (see E. S. Shaffer, *"Kubla Khan" and the Fall of Jerusalem: The Mythological School in Biblical Criticism and Secular Literature 1770-1880* [Cambridge University Press, 1975]).

In the early twentieth century, critics turned their attention to genre, and many studies attempted to classify biblical literature into such traditional categories as narrative, lyric, drama, and folklore. A pioneer in this approach was Richard Moulton, who produced both a study (*The Literary Study of the Bible,* 1899) and an anthology (*The Modern Reader's Bible,* 1926) emphasizing the generic approach. The romantic attitude also continued; it can be seen even at midcentury in Mary Ellen Chase's *The Bible and the Common Reader* (Macmillan, 1952). Chase's work—now often considered dated and superficial— preferred sweeping evaluative generalizations to pointed critical inter- pretations (for example: "The best letters ever written are in the Bible, and St. Paul is the author of them, a more vivid letter writer than even Horace Walpole or Lord Chesterfield, largely because he had far more important things than they to say"). Frequently earlier twentieth-cen- tury critics tried to separate literary from religious approaches by claiming that, whatever else it may be, the Bible is *also* great literature. Typical is this comment from the foreword to Kathleen Innes's 1930 study, *The Bible as Literature:* "Mrs. Innes had kept strictly to her chosen path, and has avoided theological or critical entanglements."

The twentieth century also produced a number of writers skeptical of literary analysis. T. S. Eliot, in his essay "Religion and Literature" (1935), argued that while it is possible to appreciate the literary merits of the Bible, those who enjoy it solely as literature (Eliot referred pri- marily to those who praise its literary style as "a monument of English prose") are essentially parasites; "the Bible has had a *literary* influ- ence," he wrote, ". . . *not* because it has been considered as literature, but because it has been considered as the report of the Word of God." C. S. Lewis also doubted that Scripture could be read "as literature" apart from an appreciation of its sacredness (see his essay "The Lit- erary Impact of the Authorised Version," 1950).

Such antagonistic views are not limited to literary people or to ear- lier decades. Biblical scholars often remain unsympathetic. James Ku- gel's important book *The Idea of Biblical Poetry: Parallelism and Its History* (Yale University Press, 1981), for example, contends that the distinction between biblical poetry and prose (often accentuated by line arrangements in modern translations) is overemphasized. He con- cludes by questioning the validity of most literary reading of the Bible: "After all, one does not read the U.S. Constitution as literature, or . . . Poor Richard's Almanac, or the Federal Reserve's Monthly Bulletin as literature. . . . [Even if we detect literary elements in such writing] we will seem to imply about the nature of the text and how it was written something that we actually believe to be untrue, or at least irrelevant. So with the Bible."

On the other hand, several modern writers have countered this view. D. F. Rauber produced two important journal articles in 1970 (on Ruth, in the *Journal of Biblical Literature;* on Jonah, in the *Bible Today*) each arguing strongly that the Bible must be read as literature. Robert Alter's series of articles in *Commentary* developed into a book, *The Art of Biblical Narrative* (Basic Books, 1981), which urges both explicitly and by demonstration a closer attention to literary nuances, an approach Alter sees as anything but antagonistic toward a religious appreciation of the text. "To scrutinize biblical personages as fictional characters," he writes, "is to see them more sharply in the multifaceted, contradictory aspects of their human individuality, which is the biblical God's chosen medium for His experiment with Israel and history." And Northrop Frye, perhaps this century's most influential critic, has repeatedly argued—most recently in *The Great Code* (Harcourt Brace Jovanovich, 1982)—that the Bible, as the mythological framework for Western culture, is itself an imaginative work that deserves to be studied as literature, though he cautions "the Bible is just as obviously 'more' than a work of literature, whatever 'more' means."

Perhaps the most noteworthy defenses of the Bible as literature in the last third of the twentieth century, however, are found in the various literary analyses being performed on a number of fronts. Evangelical Christians have taken to justifying and studying the aesthetic qualities of the Bible without sacrificing their view of its sacredness; they have a literary spokesperson in Leland Ryken. (See the bibliography at the end of this volume for his work and that of others listed below.) Frye's influence has invited the attention of archetypal critics who find in the Bible examples of universal patterns of experience that also surface in other literature, folklore, and myth, an approach heavily influenced by psychoanalysis (especially Carl Jung).

Erich Auerbach's now famous studies of Genesis and Mark in his *Mimesis: The Representation of Reality in Western Literature* sparked an interest in a New Critical approach concentrating on the biblical text and its internal nuances and suggestions. Such formalist studies have been undertaken by both literary critics like Kenneth Gros Louis and biblical scholars like Edwin Good (whose *Irony in the Old Testament* was called by Alter the first "book-length study in English by a professional Bible scholar that made a sustained effort to use a literary perspective."). Occasionally, such work is even performed by people with advanced training in both fields, like David Robertson (whose *The Old Testament and the Literary Critic* has unfortunately not been followed by more recent work) and Alter himself, who teaches both Hebrew and comparative literature at Berkeley.

Widespread interest in language and semiology in the mid-1970s produced a number of structuralist approaches to the Bible. Featured in the work of scholars like John Dominic Crossan, this method attempted to decode such literary objects as the parables of Jesus to uncover deep structures in the text. At the same time, feminist critics began to reexamine assumptions about Scripture and its interpretations, spearheaded by the work of Phyllis Trible, whose *God and the Rhetoric of Sexuality* studied female imagery and motifs in the Bible.

Recent literary interests are beginning to produce considerations of biblical material by deconstructionists, who look for loose threads they claim cause texts to unravel themselves, and reader-response (or subjectivist) critics, who examine the encounter between reader and text, the experience of reading itself. And there are continuing signs of an eclectic approach that tries to connect literary analyses of the Bible with studies of its religious value (besides the work of Frye and Alter, see that of Amos Wilder and Michael Fishbane) or with more traditional schools of biblical criticism (see Norman Petersen's *Literary Criticism for New Testament Critics*). This approach places the Bible as literature in what I consider its rightful place as a complement to— not a substitute for or antagonist toward—traditional theology and scholarship.

Though the phrase "Bible as literature" may be recent, the concept has a long and varied history. At different times it has drawn the attention of various "schools" of criticism, including the allegorical, aesthetic, romantic, generic, archetypal, formalist, structuralist, feminist, and, most recently, deconstructive and subjectivist. Arguments for and against such approaches continue. But throughout most of the long history of literary criticism there has been at least an underlying recognition that the Bible, whatever else we may say of it, often communicates with us as literature does. When we undertake literary analysis of the Bible today, we participate in a long-standing and continuing tradition inspired by this amazing book.

A map of the Holy Land, from Abraham Ortelius' "Theatrum Orbis Terrarum," 1570

The Hebrew Bible
(Old Testament)

I

Reading the Bible as Literature: The Story of the Flood

(Genesis 6–9)

As we come to examine the biblical text itself, we need to consider the kind of literary approach we will use. Let's start by backing up a moment to examine two traditional *nonliterary* ways to study the Bible and see how our approach relates to them.

I'm going to call the first the *spiritual* approach. It is used in various ways by clergy, theologians, and ordinary readers, but its intent is usually to explain or clarify the religious experience of present-day people. So a minister might see in the Flood story a revelation of divine punishment and salvation: as God punished the wicked with the destruction of the Flood and saved the righteous Noah and his family, so will he treat humanity today. A theologian might see in the strange account of the Nephilim (Gen. 6:1–4) support for her religion's doctrine of a War in Heaven precipitated by fallen angels (perhaps suggested here by "the sons of God") who became devils that still plague men and women. A lay reader might find consolation in viewing the Ark as a symbol of his church: a community singled out by God for special protection and blessing. As important and widespread as this spiritual approach is, however, it is *not* a method we will emphasize in our study.

A second traditional approach to the Bible is the *historical*— until very recently, the predominant methodology of biblical scholars. Its primary intent is to explain or clarify something about the past. So one scholar might compare what he finds in Genesis to other ancient flood stories, such as that in the Sumerian *Epic of Gilgamesh*. Another might explain apparent inconsistencies in the text by hypothesizing two or more original Flood stories that were merged into our present narrative. A third might investigate evidence for historical floods said to have afflicted the ancient Near

3

East. Such work is exciting and often immensely helpful to modern readers, but again, it is not a method we will employ.

Our approach to the Bible will be a *literary* one: we will examine the text as a source of insights into human experience as suggested by the techniques of literature. We will study the Bible, in short, to help clarify our understanding of timeless phenomena people have wrestled with both in the past *and* today: the nature of heroism, moral dilemmas, human suffering, interpersonal relationships, and—yes—the struggle with faith and the divine.

As with the spiritual and historical approaches, there are a number of options before us, even if we confine ourselves to twentieth-century literary analysis. We can follow the formalist critics in studying patterns of images, repetition, and design in the text of Gen. 6–9. We can follow archetypal critics in seeing in the Flood story an account of a primal experience of destruction and restoration—an experience that pervades, in different forms, all our lives. We can follow the more recent reader-response critics in studying the relationship between ourselves as readers and this ancient story we have probably heard and read, in one form or another, so often before. The specific approach I'm going to use is an eclectic one, borrowing from these and other sources to produce a simple, workable methodology anyone can employ to enhance his understanding of the Bible, and of himself.

There are three steps in this methodology:

1. Read the *text* as carefully as possible, distinguishing what it actually states from what we might expect it to state. As we shall see, there are many popular misconceptions about the text of the Bible that we'll have to work around.
2. Infer from the text one or more *patterns* of human experience—general ideas illustrated in the text that apply not only to the Bible's world, but to our own.
3. Use these patterns and their constituent elements to help clarify *our own experience and observation.*

To see how this works, let's examine one aspect of the Flood story: what it suggests about divinity, about the nature of the biblical God. Before turning to the process, begin with some preconceptions. When you consider the Western concept of God, what typical characteristics come to mind? My list might include the following:

—God is very powerful
—God is just
—God is merciful
—God is a loving parent
—God is awesome
—God is unchanging.

What happens to this image when we test it against the story of Noah and the Flood?

To answer, we need to turn to the first step in our process: reading the text carefully, sorting out popular misconceptions about what it states. This is often more challenging than it sounds, for unfortunately, most of us are more familiar with the Bible's reputation than with its contents. We all know, for example, that God instructs Noah to bring two of every kind of animal into the ark. And at Gen. 6:19, that is exactly what we find: "And of every living thing of all flesh, you shall bring *two* of every sort into the ark, to keep them alive with you; they shall be male and female." But when we come to 7:2, we may be surprised to find God saying, "Take with you *seven pairs* of all clean animals, the male and his mate; and *a pair* of the animals that are not clean, the male and his mate." How many pairs is it to be: one or seven? Perhaps the former, for a few verses later we read that every kind of animal, clean and unclean, goes into the ark with Noah, *"two and two, male and female"* (vv. 8–9). But the fact is, different instructions have been given. A careful reading must take this into account.

Similarly, most of us know that after the Flood, God sets a rainbow in the sky as a sign that he will never so destroy the earth again—a sign, I used to think, to remind humanity of the promise. But in fact, Genesis tells us the bow is there to remind *God:* "When I bring clouds over the earth and the bow is seen in the clouds, *I* will remember my covenant . . ." he says. "When the bow is in the clouds, *I* will look upon it and remember the everlasting covenant . . ." (9:14–16). Strange, but there it is. And so our first job is to read for "the facts, and just the facts"—not what everyone thinks is in the Bible, but what is actually stated there.

Step two is to infer from the text one or more patterns of experience—general observations about "universal" phenomena illustrated in the narrative. The Flood story illustrates several such patterns: about crime and punishment, the relationship between people and nature, between people and God. We are focusing on one—the nature of the divine—to see what it can teach us about an aspect of experience.

What do we learn about the biblical God from reading this narrative? (Remember: we are talking here only about Gen. 6–9. Many other things about God will be suggested elsewhere in the Bible.) One of the first things I notice is that God does indeed demonstrate great power. He can destroy: he annihilates nearly the whole earth and most of its inhabitants. He can save: he preserves the lives of Noah, his family, and the creatures with him in the ark. And he can replenish: after the Flood, he sees to it that the earth is restored, its inhabitants given a second chance. Clearly, there is a great deal this God can do, and no indication of limits on his power.

What about justice? Notice how God in this narrative seems just in at least one sense: he punishes wrongdoing and rewards righteousness. The Flood itself is sent in response to human corruption (Gen. 6:5–8). After it is over, God indicates he will still require satisfaction, for example, for murder: "Whoever sheds the blood of man, by man shall his blood be shed; for God made man in his own image" (9:6). On the other hand, God also rewards righteousness: he saves Noah from the Flood, he says, because "I have seen that you are righteous before me in this generation" (7:1). Clearly, this God is concerned with at least retributive justice.

On the question of mercy, however, I find the pattern of the Flood story more ambiguous. Mercy, to me, means showing kindness to one who doesn't deserve it. Does God show this quality here? Noah is saved, remember, because he is good. His family is also spared, but we don't know anything about their behavior one way or the other; perhaps this is mercy, perhaps not. There may be

6

a clearer sign in God's decision after the Flood never again to destroy all life in that way: "I will never again curse the ground because of man, for the imagination of man's heart is evil from his youth; neither will I ever again destroy every living creature as I have done" (8:21). If God means he will never again destroy *humanity* despite its innate evil, he is indeed showing mercy. But is this what he has promised? He says he will never curse the *ground,* nor destroy *every* living creature. Is this mercy, or recognition of an earlier injustice in his decision to wipe out not only people, but animals and birds—because of *human* wickedness (see 6:5–7)? Even in his later restatement—"I establish my covenant with you, that never again shall *all flesh* be cut off by the waters of a flood, and never again shall there be a flood to destroy the *earth*" (9:11)—ambiguity remains. At the least, divine mercy seems less clear here than divine justice.

To return to a clearer point, notice how God, in this narrative, resembles a loving parent in establishing a personal relationship with at least one human being. He speaks directly to Noah, seems personally involved with and concerned about him. Yet remember that Noah's *righteousness* has won the Lord's favor. Also notice how their relationship takes the form of a contractual arrangement: both before (6:18) and after (9:8–11) the Flood, God speaks of a *covenant* he will establish with Noah whereby he will promise never again to destroy all flesh. For his part, Noah is assigned a number of tasks reemphasizing his dominion over the earth (9:1–7). There is a sense that God's role as parent, while never devoid of the personal touch, also has the aura of a business arrangement. Indeed, he will continue to establish such covenants with other figures throughout much of the Bible.

We come next to the whole matter of God's personal qualities. Certainly much of what he is and does here is awesome. But notice the smaller touches, the anthropomorphic qualities that are never totally absent from the Bible. The Lord *smells* the soothing odor of Noah's sacrifice (8:21). More interesting, he appears prone to forgetfulness: he reminds *himself* not to destroy the earth by flood again, placing the rainbow in the sky as a sign to *him* (9:16–17), a kind of string tied around his finger. And there is that strange story of the Nephilim (6:1–4) with its references to "the sons of God," suggesting the Lord as a kind of family man. There is awesomeness, yes, but it is intermingled with strange personal qualities, producing an air of mystery, a sense that this God can never be fully described or pinned down.

Finally, there is the concept of God as unchanging. At the very least, this notion needs refinement in light of the Flood story. To begin with, there's the matter of those differing instructions to Noah, who is told to bring into the ark first two of every animal (6:19), then fourteen of some and two of others (7:2), and who winds up bringing two of everything (7:8–9), with no objection from God. The Lord seems to change his mind; he is certainly vacillating, if not downright confusing, about all this. More important, notice 6:6–7: "And the Lord was sorry that he had made man on the earth, and it grieved him to his heart. So the Lord said, 'I will blot out man whom I have created from the face of the ground, man and beast and creeping things and birds of the air, for I am sorry that I have made them." Clearly, God is capable of a change of heart, of doing something, then regretting it. His later decision to never again punish the ground and every living creature (8:21–22) shows that he is even prone to doubling back on, or at least refining, that change of heart itself. In these senses, the Lord is more flexible than unchanging.

Such changes suggest a related element in the pattern of divinity here: God works in cycles. He destroys and re-creates, in a death-rebirth kind of way. Notice how the Flood not only threatens to destroy the earth but to return it to the watery chaos from which creation emerged (cf. Gen. 1:1–2). But in chapter 9, God establishes a new beginning, a new creation, with clear echoes of the first creation. There are instructions to "be fruitful and multiply," and to dominate all the earth (9:1ff; cf. 1:28). There is a restrictive commandment, and even a threat of punishment (vv. 4–6; cf. 2:16–17). True, there are subtle changes (God now gives humans "every moving thing that lives" for food, for example, whereas earlier he had assigned only vegetation—9:3; cf. 1:29), but there are clear parallels as well. God has brought his universe through the cycle of near-annihilation and renewal, establishing a rhythm that will reverberate through the rest of the Bible.

So I find a pattern of divinity in the Flood narrative composed of elements ranging from extreme power to flexibility mixed with cyclic rhythms. What remains is the final step in our process—the most difficult, but most rewarding, of all. We need to use this pattern to help illuminate and clarify our own thinking and experience. We can do this by examining how the pattern's elements relate to our preconceptions about the nature of the biblical God.

As I approach this step, I discover that some of my preconceptions have been borne out: God is indeed very powerful here and quite just (at least in the sense of punishments and rewards). Others are not as clearly supported: the question of mercy, as we have seen, seems more ambiguous. (This is not to say God will not show clearer mercy elsewhere in the Hebrew Bible.) Still others are supported, but with twists or additions I hadn't thought of: so God is a loving parent of sorts, but one who can introduce a covenant, a business contract, into the family; God is awesome, but not without anthropomorphic qualities. And some preconceptions are challenged and replaced by other notions: the God of the Flood story is not unchanging but flexible, working in cycles to bring his creation to near-annihilation and then to renewal.

Must I automatically accept these "new ideas"? Certainly not. For one thing, I need to remember that the total biblical depiction of God will go well beyond these few chapters. And the whole question of how this depiction relates to reality—an important and complex issue—depends on my religious perspective. But by sifting through the ideas, I learn something. Whether it becomes part of my religious experience or simply helps me better understand the tradition I live within, it is a valuable lesson, one made possible by reading the Bible as literature.

This, then, is how we'll approach the Bible. Of course, we won't always follow the steps so formally and mechanically. Most of the time I'll assume you've read the text carefully before turning to this book. And sometimes I'll talk about our own experience *before* discussing patterns, even though clarifying that experience is the "last" step in the process. (What I like to do, in fact, is what we've done here: start by examining preconceptions about an aspect of experience, then read the text to infer one of its patterns, then use those patterns to help rethink preconceptions.) For the fact is that

9

the steps in this process are not rigid. You may want to start by using them in order, but soon you'll discover yourself reading the biblical text and being reminded of something in your own life, before you've had time to identify a pattern. Or while wrestling with how to define a pattern, you'll come upon a detail in the text that even your "careful" reading overlooked. There's no problem here; the method is adaptable to such modifications.

The important thing is that this is a method that is simple and that works. Most important, it uses the biblical text to help us discover insights about ourselves and our world, no matter what our religious convictions. We'll see more of how it works in the following chapters.

II

Moses:
The Nature of the Hero

*(Exodus 1–20; 32–34; Numbers 20;
Deuteronomy 34)*

As I move through life I encounter many people labelled "heroic."
As a child I fantasized over the exploits of Superman, Batman,
Wonder Woman. As an adult I've marveled at the life struggles of
Socrates, Joan of Arc, Martin Luther King. As a Bible reader I'm
impressed by the stories of David, Jesus, Paul.

But what makes a person heroic? Can we use these brief lists to
determine qualities shared by all or most heroes? Certainly some
common elements appear immediately. All of these heroes—real
and imaginary—have had to struggle against incredible odds, for
example. Many took on the establishments of their times, becoming subjects of controversy. Several died as martyrs for a cause.
Most had legends develop about them, making it difficult to separate fact from distortion.

The story of Moses, it seems to me, is no exception. Here is a
biblical hero who struggles to free his people from powerful slave-
lords, who takes on the mighty Egyptian Pharaoh, who loses his
life in the quest for his people's homeland, whose reputation is not
always consistent with what the text tells us about him. Perhaps a
closer look at these few chapters (his complete story winds
throughout the books from Exodus to Deuteronomy) will help
sharpen our understanding of heroism, for a great many of Moses'
heroic traits parallel those of heroes in popular culture, in history,
and elsewhere in the Bible.

There is an example in the story of Moses' birth in Exod. 2. In
many ancient cultures, the hero's life is threatened near birth, and
he must be hidden from danger. In Greek mythology, Dionysius's
mother, Semele, is killed, and the yet-unborn child must be rescued

11

and hidden in the thigh of his father, Zeus. In the New Testament, the infant Jesus is "hidden" in Egypt to protect him from Herod's wrath (see Matt. 2). And in the Ancient Near East, there are many stories of young heroes saved in this way; Sargon of Akkad (ca. 2300 B.C.E.), for example, was placed in a basket of reeds and floated on a river, later to be rescued. The famous story of the infant Moses being placed in a basket near the Nile clearly fits this model of the hero's infant susceptibility.

Consider several other elements in the life of the typical hero and note the extent to which Moses fills the bill. (My analysis is inspired by, and partly modeled after, David Leeming's *Mythology: The Voyage of the Hero,* which finds several definable stages in the hero's life—only some, however, explicitly related to Moses.) There is, for example, the matter of initiation: the young hero is tested and introduced to the world of experience. So the boy David slays Goliath (1 Sam. 17), twelve-year-old Jesus converses learnedly in the Temple (Luke 2:41–51), the future King Arthur removes the magic sword Excalibur from a rock.

I find Moses' initiation in his two early opportunities to defend underdogs against bullies. Encountering an Egyptian beating an enslaved Hebrew, Moses instinctively sides with his own people and kills the Egyptian. He soon learns, however, that the news has spread and so flees for his life (Exod. 2:11–15). Arriving at Midian, he rescues the daughters of the Midianite priest from shepherds who have driven them from a well (vv. 16–22). In each case the hero's mettle is tested, and he learns that actions have consequences both bad and good, for in the first instance, Pharaoh does indeed seek Moses' life (v. 15), but in the second, the priest gives him a daughter in marriage (v. 21).

Many heroes also experience withdrawal: they remove themselves from society for a time, to plan, meditate, or—whether by design or accident—simply grow up. Superman frequents his Fortress of Solitude, young Dionysius wanders through strange lands before returning to his own country, Jesus spends forty days and nights in the wilderness (for example, Matt. 4:1–11). Moses' retreat to Midian is such a withdrawal for him, for he settles there without noting the groans and cries of his people in Egypt—appeals that are, however, heard and responded to by God (2:23–25). Indeed, God will have to call Moses out of seclusion, leading to the next stage in his heroic life.

And that stage is inspiration: the hero is singled out and overpowered by a force that transcends the human. So the Holy Spirit descends upon Jesus at his baptism (Matt. 3:13–17), and Paul is converted by a dramatic vision on the road to Damascus (Acts 9:1–9). As in these later cases, the moment of inspiration for Moses is a theophany: a manifestation of the deity. It is the incident at the burning bush (Exod. 3:1–6)—a religious experience marked by mystery (how can a bush burn and not consume itself?) and wonder (Moses says "I will turn aside and see this great sight, why the bush is not burnt"), exuding a sense of the sacred (God tells Moses, "Do not come near; put off your shoes from your feet, for the place on which you are standing is holy ground"), and a sense of fear (Moses hides his face, afraid to look at God). It is an event that will change the course of the hero's life and the fate of his people.

The next heroic trait I find in Moses may seem surprising, for it is a "negative" quality not popularly identified with heroism. I'm speaking of reluctance: the hero's unwillingness to assume his role, his need to be pushed into it. We find it in Odysseus, for example, who tries to avoid service in the Greek army by feigning insanity: when the enlistment officers come they discover him sowing salt instead of seed in the field, and only by throwing his infant son before the plow, forcing him to turn aside, can they be sure their man has his wits about him. We find it, too, in Martin Luther, who resisted attempts to break openly with Rome until mounting circumstances forced him to take his stand.

Moses' reluctance to respond to his God is persistent. First he invokes humility: "Who am I that I should go to Pharaoh, and bring the sons of Israel out of Egypt?" (3:11). When God promises divine aid, Moses pleads ignorance: "If I come to the people of Israel and say to them, 'The God of your fathers has sent me to you,' and they ask me, 'What is his name?' what shall I say to them?" (v. 13). When God explains his name. Moses turns to another excuse: lack of credentials. "But behold, they will not believe me or listen to my voice," he complains, "for they will say, 'The

Lord did not appear to you'" (4:1). And when God provides the credentials by empowering Moses to perform miracles, our hero bemoans his personal weakness: "Oh, my Lord, I am not eloquent . . . ; but I am slow of speech and of tongue" (v. 10). This tries God's patience and enkindles his anger (v. 14), and when God suggests Moses' brother Aaron as spokesperson, Moses dare not refuse again. Still, he has made every attempt to wheedle out of his duties, and only divine persistence, patience, and anger have pushed him into it.

His reluctance overcome, Moses is ready to demonstrate another facet of heroism: possession of special powers. Most heroes can perform superhuman feats or even miracles. Sometimes these show physical prowess (Wonder Woman saves an innocent child from certain destruction; Samson brings down the house upon the Philistines—Judg. 16:28–31), sometimes mental skill (Oedipus solves the mysterious riddle of the Sphinx; Cassandra accurately predicts the future). Moses' feats are of both types (he can bring plagues upon the Egyptians and stubbornly outwit Pharaoh), but they can be subsumed under one heading: his ability to serve as the Lord's agent. This is most clearly seen in the plagues. They are obviously the result of special power: though the early miracles are easily duplicated by Egyptian magicians (Exod. 7:22), Moses' work quickly surpasses their ability (8:18). Yet the most persistent note about this power is that it is literally superhuman: the Lord, working through Moses and Aaron, is the Hebrew magician. Ironically, the trait we perhaps most popularly associate with heroism—this possession of special powers—is one Moses can hardly call his own. Like at least some other figures (Cassandra, whose predictions are the work of Apollo; Samson, whose strength also comes from the Lord), he has powers that emanate from the divine.

Nonetheless, it is likely these special powers, human or divine, that help Moses illustrate another characteristic: the hero is often subject to vacillating reputation. Sometimes he is condemned by his contemporaries and enshrined only generations after death. (So Joan of Arc is first executed, then later declared a saint, by the same institution.) In other cases he is treated inconsistently even in his own time; the crowd is fickle, rallying to him when he offers what they want, turning against him when things get rough. (So Jesus is at times enthusiastically supported, at other times nearly stoned, by the crowds.) I find at least the latter phenomenon in Moses' story. The same Israelites who gladly follow him out of Egypt when he promises freedom quickly turn rebellious and blame him for upsetting the status quo: "What have you done to us, in bringing us out of Egypt? Is not this what we said to you in Egypt, 'Let us alone and let us serve the Egyptians'?" (14:11–12; when did this fickle people ever utter those words?). Repeatedly throughout the journey, the masses will clamor for food and water, will long for "the fleshpots of Egypt," will blame Moses and Aaron for their hardship. Yet just as quickly will they again follow their leaders and hide behind them in their fear. "You speak to us, and we will hear," they say to Moses after the dramatic presentation of the Ten Commandments, "but let not God speak to us, lest we die" (20:19). Like many a hero, Moses must bear the vicissitudes of reputation, must repeatedly test his patience against fickle followers.

Which leads to another dimension of heroism: the hero often represents a cause larger than himself. So Elijah fights as prophet of Yahweh against the priests of the Canaanite god Baal (1 Kings 18:20–40), and Martin Luther King symbolizes a civil-rights movement. Moses' larger cause is twofold. At times he is clearly an agent of the Lord, a prophet who serves as intermediary between the divine and the human. Yet in other instances, the cause he represents is his people, Israel itself. After the incident of the golden calf, for instance, the Lord is angry enough to want to destroy this nation: "let me alone, that my wrath may burn hot against them and I may consume them," he tells Moses. But the prophet beseeches his God, invoking the promises made to the patriarchs, and convinces the Lord to change his mind (Exod. 32:9–14). Whether representing his God or his nation, then, this hero is called upon to selflessly devote his life to a larger cause.

And in so devoting himself, Moses takes on a different heroic quality: he acquires an air of mystery, of otherness, a fearful, lonely quality that sets him apart from the crowd. It is a quality shared on one level by Batman, whose costume, mask, and secret identity produce it, on another by Cassandra, isolated by her ability to fore-tell the future, on yet another by Jesus, transfigured mysteriously before his followers' eyes (Mark 9:2–8). The Hebrew word for "holiness"—qodesh—suggests this kind of otherness. I find hints of it in Moses' increasing tendency to speak to the Lord alone, while others wait apart; in one instance, he is unaware of the glow his face has taken on from the divine presence, a glow producing fear in his followers and ultimately leading him to veil his face, a physical symbol of his separation (34:29–35). Like the narrator of Coleridge's "Kubla Khan," of whom the people say

> Weave a circle round him thrice,
> And close your eyes with holy dread,
> For he on honeydew hath fed,
> And drunk the milk of Paradise,

Moses, and heroes like him, exude a quality that mysteriously tempers admiration with fear.

Finally, we come to the quality that, despite all else, keeps the hero within our grasp. There are limits on these people, weaknesses that make them vulnerable, that prevent their becoming gods. Superman, despite his prowess, is susceptible to kryptonite; Noah, despite his righteousness, lies in a drunken stupor, naked in his tent (Gen. 9:21). Moses, too, remains always human. He may speak to the Lord as others do not, he may even watch as the Lord passes by (33:17–23)—but he cannot see the divine face, for, God tells him, "man shall not see me and live" (v. 20). And man Moses will always be. Indeed, in a later part of his story, his humanity erupts into a fateful misjudgment, a kind of tragic flaw. In Num. 20, when the Israelites cry out for water, God instructs Moses and Aaron to speak to a rock so it will yield its water before their eyes. But the brothers, frustrated by the pestering of their people, upbraid them in anger, and Moses strikes the rock twice with his staff, instead of speaking to it. This infringement is enough to kindle divine wrath, and the Lord says, "Because you did not believe in me, to sanctify me in the eyes of the people of Israel, therefore you shall not bring this assembly into the land which I have given them" (v. 12). And indeed, both Moses and Aaron die before the Exodus is over, punished for their all-too-human transgression. Like most heroes, they, too, have feet of clay.

The story of Moses, then, suggests to me at least ten characteristics of the hero: infant susceptibility, initiation, withdrawal, inspiration, reluctance, possession of special powers, vacillating reputation, subjection to a larger cause, mystery, and human limitations. We have seen how these traits mark the lives of many heroes. Yet perhaps in a wider sense, they mark our lives as well. Does not infant susceptibility, for instance, promote the almost universal tendency of parents to cuddle and "hide" their young, to protect them from adversity? Do not we all undergo initiation, even if it takes the mundane form of passing through school or surviving a driver's examination? Do not vacations, retreats, sabbaticals, illustrate the same human need for periodic renewal and reflection that leads the heroes to withdrawal?

In short, the lives of the heroes may be our lives, too, the distinctions between them and us differences of degree, not kind. And so reading the story of Moses provides insights, not just about a special group of individuals, but about our very selves.

III

Jephtah:
The Moral Dilemma

(Judges 11)

A Jehovah's Witness must choose between a blood transfusion for his dying child and a religious conviction forbidding that transfusion. A mother must decide whether or not to pull the plug on her comatose daughter. A father holding a gun on his berserk drug-addicted son must quickly decide whether to squeeze the trigger. Each of these people confronts a moral dilemma: an impossible choice, in these cases between the welfare—indeed, the life or death—of their offspring and other values like religion, the alleviation of suffering, the protection of a neighborhood. Such dilemmas are all around us, and they're not confined to unusual, highly dramatic moments: the parents who choose, consciously or not, between time for their children and time for their professions are dealing with a similar problem.

Moral dilemmas affecting children are a popular theme in ancient literature: Agamemnon must decide whether to sacrifice his daughter Iphigenia or risk the fury of a goddess, and Abraham confronts an analogous situation when God tells him to sacrifice "your son, your only son Isaac, whom you love" (Gen. 22:2). A third example is Jephtah, a little-known figure in the Book of Judges who, having rashly vowed to sacrifice the first living creature to emerge from his door upon his return from battle, sees his only daughter run out to greet him and must choose whether to honor that vow or not. His decision is immediate and unequivocal: the girl must die. It remains for us to decide if he acts rightly.

Like dilemmas involving children, the rash vow is also found throughout literature, and history too. Oedipus vows to curse King Laius's murderer if Apollo will lift a plague from his city, never dreaming the murderer is himself. Luther vows to become a priest if God will spare him from a savage storm, hardly foreseeing the

18

consequences for himself and for Christianity. Such vows are marked by unintended ambiguity (Laius's murderer could be any-body; becoming a priest can mean many things) that only becomes clear in the ironic upshot (included among "anybody" is Oedipus himself; included within "becoming a priest" is reforming/breaking from the Catholic church).

Like these figures, Jephtah makes a promise upon a condition, little realizing the end result. He tells the Lord, "If thou wilt give the Ammonites into my hand, then whoever comes forth from the doors of my house to meet me, when I return victorious from the Ammonites, shall be the Lord's, and I will offer him up for a burnt offering" (Judg. 11:30–31). The ambiguity reverberates through Jephtah's word *whoever,* though his later pronoun *him* ("I will of-fer *him* up") clearly implies he is not thinking of his daughter. The ironic upshot is here mixed with pathos; so when the girl, knowing nothing of the vow, comes out to celebrate her father's victory "with timbrels and with dances," and when we read "she was his only child; beside her he had neither son nor daughter" (v. 34)—a line that echoes "your son, your only son Isaac, whom you love"— Jephtah's anguish is understandable. But none of this should ob-scure the central question: does he do the right thing in killing his daughter? It is a classic dilemma, for not to kill is to violate a sacred vow (see Deut. 23:21–23), yet to kill is to perform an abhorrent act forbidden in Israel (see Exod. 13:13; Lev. 18:21). We need to consider both sides of the argument, but first, I want to establish two premises.

Premise one: I want to undertake a moral evaluation, not a legal or theological one. The question of how Israelite law would judge Jephtah's act (which is more important: the duty to fulfill a vow or the ban on human sacrifice?) is intriguing, but beyond my scope here. The question of how Jephtah's God would judge the act is also important, but not an issue for me to decide. I want to focus on the moral rightness or wrongness of what he has done. These are three separate questions (I will argue later that moral and the-ological judgments, in particular, must sometimes be distin-guished), and the one I've chosen to deal with is the moral one.

Premise two: the moral standards I will use are my own. Again, it is valuable to consider how Jephtah's contemporaries would have judged him, but I am not his contemporary. It is my own standards I am interested in identifying, refining, and testing (recognizing that among those standards I may want to *consider* the ethical codes of Jephtah and his world). Within the literary pattern I hope to examine in this narrative are a series of moral questions that should enlighten judgments I make about *my* contemporaries—and about myself. So I will not try to judge as "they" might have judged, but as I might.

To return, then, to the central question. None can deny the deed: Jephtah does slay his daughter. Few can deny its horror: even the narrative cannot bear to be explicit about it, telling us only that he "did with her according to his vow which he had made" (v. 39). But in moral terms, using my standards, is he right? Let's begin with the side that says he is, with his moral defense. I want to examine four arguments here, along the way identifying and questioning key assumptions on which each is based.

The first argument is subtle yet important: Jephtah is innocent because his own unsettled background excuses, or at least mitigates responsibility for, his rash statements and acts. To be sure, his background is decidedly unsettled. His parentage is ambiguous and tainted: he is the illegitimate son of Gilead—a generic name for a district, not a person—and a prostitute (11:1). His father's legitimate sons taunt him and send him away to a land where "worthless fellows" gather round him to form raiding parties (vv. 2–3). Yet when trouble brews, the elders of Gilead turn to their rejected countryman, practicing an inconsistency Jephtah is quick to note: "Did you not hate me, and drive me out of my father's house? Why have you come to me now when you are in trouble?" (v. 7). (There is, by the way, a clear parallel between the way the people treat Jephtah and the inconsistency of their relationship to Yahweh; compare 10:6–16.)

All of which raises an important point: in making a moral judgment, to what extent do we consider such extenuating circumstances? In assessing an accused murderer's responsibility, do we weigh the fact that she is the product of a broken home and confused childhood? On one level we certainly must, and yet, it seems to me, such circumstances add up more to an explanation than to an excuse. Life is tough all over—tougher for some, to be sure, than others—yet ultimately, don't we need to take responsibility for our own actions, to quit blaming family and upbringing? Moreover, it seems clear that, despite his background, Jephtah is not incapable of rational behavior: his long, reasoned speech to the Ammonites (11:15–27) on the justness of Israel's claim to disputed territory shows that the battle he wages against them is not an unthought-out attack. This argument from Jephtah's background seems to me to do little to exonerate him from blame for killing his daughter.

But there is more. Some might claim Jephtah slays justifiably because he has struck a bargain with the Lord, who has fulfilled his obligation by delivering the Ammonites into Jephtah's hand. For the judge not to follow through would be gross sacrilege, and Jephtah says as much at 11:35: "I have opened my mouth to the Lord, and I cannot take back my vow." I have a problem with this reasoning, however. It assumes that his vow is valid and binding. But in fact, is it not rash and foolishly ambiguous? As we have seen, Jephtah has promised "whoever comes forth from the doors of my house" (the Hebrew says "the one coming forth who comes forth," an ambiguity preserved in the New English Bible's rendering "the first creature that comes out of the door"). He was indeed unwise to utter the vow, but to what extent can we expect someone to fulfill such a promise, made on the eve of battle, when it is certain he did not intend the eventual outcome? However foolish the vow may have been, is it necessary to compound the wrong by going through with the horrible deed?

But we are still not done. Defenders of Jephtah might well argue that as a judge, a leader of Israel, he is duty-bound to exemplify strict devotion to the Lord; to violate a vow would hardly set a proper example. True, but again the argument is based on a noteworthy assumption: that fulfilling *this* vow demonstrates devotion to the Lord. Whose idea was the vow, anyway? Does it not appear to be Jephtah's (see 11:30–31 again)? In Gen. 22 it was God who started the ball rolling, God who instructed Abraham to sacrifice Isaac. There are no such instructions here. The killing of his daughter seems Jephtah's doing from beginning to end; if so, it hardly illustrates devotion to his God.

Which leads to a final argument on this side of the issue: that Jephtah must slay his daughter because, like Oedipus, he must accept responsibility for bringing this evil on himself, must be willing to shoulder the consequences of his vow. This is a noble sentiment indeed, and I'm all for the notion of individual responsibility—but hold on. Is Jephtah's vow *fully* his? Just before he utters it we read "Then the Spirit of the Lord came upon" him (11:29). Is God behind the vow—and thus the killing—after all? I know, I just finished arguing that divine instructions are absent here, and that's true: there are no *instructions*. But divine *influence*? I find the narrative ambiguous on this score, reminding me that these issues are never as simple as they appear. Moreover, there's another assumption to be tested. To say that Jephtah must accept responsibility for his promise implies that no other human being is involved in what he "must" do. But it is Jephtah's daughter, not the judge himself, who will give up her life. He may be smitten with anguish; she will be smitten with death. Is it morally right to ask one person to die that another might shoulder responsibilities with integrity?

In short, though Jephtah's slaying of his daughter is not without moral defense—he *is* the product of an unsettled background, he *has* struck a bargain with the Lord, he *is* a leader whose devotion to God should set an example, he *must* be ready to accept the consequences of his behavior—each defense rests on assumptions that I've found cause to question. What about the other side of the case? Let's now examine three arguments *for* Jephtah's moral guilt, again testing underlying assumptions.

First, the whole mess seems to have started with Jephtah's vow, making him responsible, it would appear, for all that follows. If the vow was foolish and ambiguous, it was he who made it so. He cannot even claim he made it "under pressure," since he uttered it *before* the conflict with the Ammonites, not in the heat of battle. He should have thought of consequences beforehand. And yet there is that ambiguity already noted: having been overtaken by "the Spirit of the Lord," did Jephtah in truth make the vow himself? Moreover, a bargain with the Lord, even a rash one, is serious business; whatever its foolishness, can a person simply refuse to comply out of hand?

A second argument for Jephtah's guilt is this: he has taken the life of, not any victim, but his own daughter—indeed, his only child. Perhaps the law makes no distinction, but morally, he has violated one of the most fundamental human bonds: it is a parent's obligation to nurture and protect a child, not to slay her. Again, however, I detect a hidden assumption: that protecting his child is a parent's *highest* obligation. If a father's pistol is all that stands between his drug-crazed, gun-wielding son and certain death for others, is the father wrong to pull the trigger? True, Jephtah's daughter threatens no one, but the example illustrates that there are sometimes higher values than the life of one's child. Throughout the Hebrew Bible, the Lord is presented as the highest value; witness the first commandment (Exod. 20:1–3). Horrible as child-slaying may be, perhaps there are cases—including this one— where it becomes necessary.

But there is still a third argument, not yet touched on at all. The killing of Jephtah's daughter is premeditated, not spontaneous. The vow may have been rash, but the killing is not: two months elapse (11:39) before the girl's life is taken. Obviously this is a planned and calculated act, a morally indefensible murder.

Yet again, untested assumptions lurk in the background. Is a premeditated killing always murder, if circumstances "require" it? If a sniper has already shot ten people and is threatening others, is the policeman who shoots and kills him a murderer? What about the warden who throws the switch for a legal execution? True, these questions are debatable, and Jephtah's situation is again not identical to them, but they remind us that large segments of our society do not categorically label all premeditated killing as murder. And what Jephtah performs, it might be said, is not a premeditated killing but a sacrifice; he makes an offering necessitated by his commitment to the Lord. As with earlier arguments, the issue is not as simple as it appears.

We seem to have come full circle. There are arguments defending Jephtah's killing, but questionable assumptions lie beneath them. There are arguments holding him morally responsible, but they rest on premises that can be challenged, too. Where do we go from here?

I think I find a way out, for myself at least, in the important distinction addressed earlier between moral and theological ethics. Things may be theologically right but morally wrong. The father who refuses a blood transfusion for his dying child may indeed be doing what he conceives his God to ask and thus be theologically justified. The problem is that it is often hard—indeed, impossible—for the rest of us to judge theological ethics: how can I know what God will think of this father? Nonetheless, I may have to judge on the moral level, and there, I may have to say that father is wrong, theological scruples notwithstanding. I don't mean that moral values always supersede theological values, but that when the two conflict, I can only judge what I can judge. Thus when a Jim Jones argues by implication that his God ordered him to lead hundreds to mass suicide in Guyana, I have to judge him morally wrong—recognizing with vexation that in a theological court the verdict may be different.

This is the reasoning that leads me to say Jephtah is morally wrong for slaying his daughter. Arguments in his defense can be challenged, as I have tried to show. Arguments against him also seem assailable, but attacks on them all appear to me to rest on the notion that Jephtah is doing what he conceives his God to be asking. Though his vow may be foolish, his support seems to say, either it is divinely inspired in the first place, or it places him under an obligation to the Lord from which he cannot escape. Though he violates a familial bond in slaying his child, he does so because of a higher obligation to his God. Though his act is indeed premeditated, it is again necessitated by his overwhelming obligation to put that God first. Granted all this, Jephtah's defense rests on a matter between his God and himself, a relationship I find impossible to judge. Even in this text, God is strangely silent about his own view of Jephtah's behavior. And so though the man may indeed be doing what he perceives is right, and on one level may even be right in thinking so, I have to judge him morally wrong.

Making moral judgments is a difficult but essential part of living. Certainly some will disagree with my conclusions. But the important thing is to examine the reasoning, to test, challenge, and evaluate it. For this literary text has again suggested to me a pattern, this time of ethical issues involved in making moral judgments. Does one's upbringing provide an explanation or an excuse for later behavior? Must one be expected to follow through on a bad vow? Does a religious leader exemplify devotion to his God by offering something that that God hasn't requested? Can one strive for moral integrity by sacrificing the life of another? Perhaps most important, does a belief that one is doing "what God wants" justify otherwise unethical behavior?

Such issues go well beyond the specific case of Jephtah. The pattern they comprise, and the procedures I've used—examining both sides of the question, testing assumptions, distinguishing moral from theological or legal concerns—have helped me arrive at a personal conclusion about him, but more important, they enlighten my thinking about real situations ranging from the Guyana tragedy to the cases of the three parents whose dilemmas began this chapter. Literary analysis is at its best when it helps with the struggles in the real world of our own lives.

IV

Samson:
Another Slant on the Hero

(Judges 13–16)

In discussing Moses, we noted traits shared by many heroes. Such heroes serve several positive functions: they provide role models, embody cultural values, help unite and instill pride in a people. But there is another side to heroism: sometimes it gets out of hand and becomes dysfunctional.

We may, for example, pay too much attention to a hero, giving him or her an inflated sense of self-importance and moral freedom; the antics of several movie stars provide illustrations. We may enshrine certain heroes and come to admire their questionable values; some people, for instance, are enthralled by the drugs-sex-violence images of certain rock singers. Excessive hero worship causes us to lose perspective; the incredible salaries paid major sports figures seem out of line with their value to society. And such worship can blind us to what's happening; at its worst, it can produce a Hitler beyond anyone's control.

In short, though we rightfully think of them as admirable, there is another slant on heroes, one I find treated in the Samson narrative. I want to examine four points dramatized for me in this story: that traditional heroic traits (strength, vengeance, cleverness) may prove of little avail; that the real hero may be not human but divine; that the divine hero's purpose may differ from that of humans, who act out his aims unawares; that the human function in all this may be to remain faithful to the divine, for apostasy leads to temporary, though never permanent, rejection.

Samson possesses several traditional heroic traits. Perhaps most obvious is the physical strength he demonstrates repeatedly: he kills a lion bare-handed (Judg. 14:6), slays thirty men to pay off a debt (14:19), kills one thousand with the jawbone of an ass (15:15), uproots the doors of the city gate of Gaza and places them

26

atop a hill (16:3). He is a Hebrew Hercules. But what good comes of these amazing feats? Some are decidedly petty—killing thirty presumably innocent men to pay off a foolish bet! Others have at best short-term value; after each flexing of his muscles, sooner or later the Philistines solve his riddle, burn his wife and father-in-law, or capture and enslave him. In the long run, Samson's antics help neither Israel nor himself.

The same can be said for another of Samson's "heroic" traits: vengeance. It is easy to imagine how a culture might immortalize a hero who wreaks vengeance on their enemy, but Samson's avenging gets nowhere. When his wife is taken from him in chapter 15, he gets even with the Philistines (never mind that it was only the woman's father who gave her to another) by burning their fields with torches attached to foxes' tails. The Philistines respond by burning the woman and her father. Samson, now siding with his wife and father-in-law, attacks the Philistines "hip and thigh with great slaughter" (15:8). The Philistines come after Samson and the men of Judah bind and deliver him to them—but the ropes on his arms break and he slays a thousand men. The narrative then gives us a breather so we can tote up the score: this revenge has led from destruction of property, to immolation of two human beings, to mass slaughter, to betrayal, and eventually to mass slaughter again. If Samson has won out, it is surely a hollow victory; at best, he comes off like a nasty fraternity prankster, at worst, like Attila the Hun.

A third heroic trait—one Samson is not always given credit for—is cleverness. Ancient peoples saw a sign of cleverness in the ability to solve, or pose an unsolvable, riddle: Oedipus is made king of Thebes after freeing the city from a curse by solving the Sphinx's riddle. Samson's riddle—"out of the eater came something to eat / Out of the strong came something sweet" (14:14)—is good enough to stump the Philistines for a while, and they eventually solve it only by cheating. Moreover, riddles are not his only mental strength. Before Delilah finally learns his secret, Samson puts her off, not once, but three times, with clever tall tales about how he can be captured. He is not a simple "dumb ox." Yet again, his cleverness is ultimately to no avail: sooner or later he himself reveals the secrets of his riddle and his strength.

Thus I find a pattern emerging: though Samson illustrates such traditional human heroic traits as strength, vengefulness, and cleverness—traits encompassing our physical, emotional, and mental faculties—each proves of little use in the long run. Can we, then, call him a hero? This leads to point two: the real hero in this narrative is not human but divine. If Samson is "heroic," it is not because he possesses extraordinary physical, emotional, and mental qualities, but because he is given a spiritual quality—because he is specially chosen by the Lord, who stands behind him as the real driving force. Before he is born, an angel of the Lord tells Samson's mother he is to be consecrated to God from the day of his birth and "shall begin to deliver Israel from the hand of the Philistines" (13:5). It is easy to forget such a prophecy, for after chapter 13 Samson hardly seems a divine agent. Yet, it seems to me, God is there, prompting and waiting. Samson's deeds are often preceded by a visit from "the Spirit of the Lord." When he prays for a drink after the jawbone slaughter—the only time he turns to the Lord until the end of his story—God immediately and miraculously provides water (15:18–19). And when he prays again in the Philistine god Dagon's temple ("O Lord God, remember me, I pray thee, and strengthen me, I pray thee, only this once, O God, that I may be avenged upon the Philistines . . . "[16:28]), the strength that had left him returns. And so my reading of the Samson narrative emphasizes an important twist: the protagonist is not the human being with his strength, vengeance, and cleverness; that person is "heroic" only as a selected front man for the real hero, the Lord.

Point three shows me how the Lord uses his front men. The divine hero's purposes differ from those of humans; he uses humans to act out his larger aims unawares. We have seen how from the first God has chosen Samson to "begin to deliver Israel from . . . the Philistines" (13:5), and how Samson has behaved like anything but the Lord's chosen, oblivious to any service for Israel. And yet, it seems to me, the Lord uses even such an unlikely figure as this. Samson is continually motivated by his own petty instincts: he marries the woman of Timnah against his parents' wishes, for example, because she "pleases" him (14:3). But the Lord has other things in mind, as we see in the next verse: "His father and mother

28

did not know that it [the impending marriage] was from the Lord; for he was seeking an occasion against the Philistines" (14:4). Humans don't know what their God has in mind. And indeed Samson's continual squabbles with the Philistines, always instigated by his personal whims, cause them to retaliate and thus make possible the final conflict that pits, not Samson against his enemies—human against human—but Yahweh against Dagon—god against god.

Ironically, even in this great climactic scene, Samson seems unaware of the Lord's higher purpose. The Philistines are in the temple sacrificing to Dagon, taunting Yahweh with their chant: "*Our* god has given our enemy into our hand, the ravager of our country, who has slain many of us" (16:24). In a moment, Yahweh, through Samson, will vindicate himself. But Samson thinks not at all of this clash between gods. His prayer, as usual, is for his personal revenge: ". . . that I may be avenged upon the Philistines *for one of my two eyes*" (v. 28). He dies not realizing the great theological battle in which he has served. Yet that battle has been fought and won by the Lord. Human beings go their merry way, but the Lord accomplishes greater purposes with them, things they do not dream of.

If, then, human heroism doesn't work, if it is up to God to be hero, if human "heroes" don't always realize of what they are a part, what is left for people to do? I find an answer in the final point I want to make about the Samson story, a point stressed repeatedly throughout the Book of Judges. The human role is to remain faithful to the divine; to do otherwise leads to temporary, though never permanent, rejection. Samson gets away with almost every imaginable crime, from arson to dalliance with women to mass murder. He is a petty bully from start to finish. Yet the only time he really gets in trouble is when he turns from his God in allowing Delilah to shave his head and thus violate the vow imposed on him at birth (see 16:17). Not only does his strength desert him, but—for the first and only time—the Lord leaves him, too (16:20). Yet when he turns to the Lord again in the Philistine temple, his strength, and his God, return.

It has been just so with Israel. Throughout Judges, each time this people does what is wrong in the eyes of the Lord, they are abandoned to their enemies (see 13:1). But not really abandoned, for God remains in the background, ready to raise up a deliverer. That deliverer appears to be a judge; Samson, we are told, judged Israel twenty years (15:20). But the real savior has been the Lord—not a human being, but the true hero of the story. Apostasy leads to punishment, for Samson and his people, but redemption is at hand, in the Lord himself.

To the notion of heroism, then, my reading of this narrative adds a special perspective. In the world of Samson, traditional heroism—invoking physical, emotional, and mental accomplishments—gets perverted and doesn't work. Real heroism is found in the divine, not the human. The human "hero" is an unwitting tool of the divine, achieving goals of which he is not aware. And the human role is not to act heroic in the usual sense, but to remain faithful to the divine. That faithfulness is reciprocated, and a major function of the hero—to stand for his people against their enemy—fulfilled.

V

Saul:
A Tragic Hero?

(1 Samuel 8–31)

The heroine Antigone insists on giving proper burial to her brother. Defying King Creon, she boldly asserts her rights against the state's. Banished to a cave, she dies alone.

Prince Hamlet, instructed to avenge his father's death, decides to proceed with deliberate caution. His carefulness results in his undoing.

The salesman Willy Loman has bought the American dream lock, stock, and barrel. His purchase leads to his suicide.

Why have such stories permeated our culture from ancient times to the present? Are they just stories, "only" literature—or something more? Surely they touch a central chord in our experience, for such tragedies seem to have a stronger, more enduring hold on us than any other type of literature. Perhaps they remind us of life's ultimate irony: one's fall can sometimes be traced to one's strength. Antigone's steadfastness, Hamlet's caution, and Willy's dream are good in themselves, yet each leads to its possessor's ruin. And the pattern is not confined to fiction; there is something truly tragic in a Martin Luther King, for example, who in the very act of organizing a march for civil rights is struck down by an assassin's bullet.

Aristotle long ago reminded us that not every type of person is fit to be a tragic hero; it is hard to see Hitler's death as tragedy, for example, since the fall of a depraved and wicked man seems inevitable and just. We need some criteria. I suggest starting with two other points emphasized in Aristotle's classic treatise on tragedy, *The Poetics:* that a true tragic hero should experience a change of fortune from happiness to misery and should elicit the tragic emotions of fear and pity (of these, more later). I would add something hinted at, though never made explicit, in the *Poetics:* the hero's fall

31

should result in part, at least, from his strength. And I would conclude with something Aristotle doesn't mention: when the hero knows ruin is upon him, he should face his fate squarely and stoically. I would like now to test whether Saul is a tragic hero by examining his case in light of these four criteria. It seems to me that, though in each case he comes close to meeting the standard, ambiguities cloud the issue and make him fall just short of the mark.

It might seem clear enough that Saul's fortune changes from good to bad, from happiness to misery. The first thing we read about him is "There was not a man among the people of Israel more handsome [the Hebrew word can mean 'good,' in any and every sense] than he; from his shoulders upward he was taller than any of the people" (9:2; physical descriptions are rare in the Bible, so keep this one in mind). He is chosen by the Lord as first king of Israel. And by story's end, he seems much worse off: rejected by this same God, he falls his full length to the ground in fright and dies knowing with vexation he will be replaced by the more favored and successful David. By and large, a change from happiness to misery is there, and yet, it seems to me clouded. Saul's initial "happiness" is mitigated by confusion: in his first appearance he wanders aimlessly and unsuccessfully in search of his father's lost animals, depending on a servant for direction. He is not the self-assured Antigone. And his "misery," as I will try to show, may be his finest hour. The general pattern of tragic change is there, yet its impact is softened by ambiguity.

What about my second criterion: Aristotle's notion of fear and pity? This will need more extensive consideration. Fear, says Aristotle, is aroused by the suffering of "someone just like ourselves," that is, someone we can identify with because he is neither a monster of depravity nor a paragon of virtue; what happens to him could be happening to us. Pity comes from "undeserved misfortune"; we feel it for the man whose suffering exceeds what he has earned, whose fall comes about, Aristotle goes on to say, from a *hamartia*, an unfortunate decision he makes.

Where does Saul fit in all this? Let's begin by investigating whether he really is "a man like ourselves," one we can fear for and identify with because he is neither excessively wicked and depraved nor unbelievably good. On the positive side, he shows me some leadership qualities, at least in military affairs: he rallies his countrymen to a victory over the Ammonites (11:6–11) and makes his throne secure (14:47–48), acting "valiantly" and creating the job of Israelite king as he goes along. At the same time, he is humble: when first singled out for the throne he asks Samuel, "Am I not a Benjaminite, from the least of the tribes of Israel? And is not my family the humblest of all the families of Benjamin? Why then have you spoken to me in this way?" (9:21). Later, though anointed prince, we find him working in the field (11:5). He hardly seems a monster of depravity.

But there is more. Saul shows admirable restraint when, after his victory at Jabesh-Gilead, he refuses to accede to the popular demand that those who spoke against him be killed (11:12–15). And he demonstrates honor: when an oath he had uttered is unwittingly violated by Jonathon, he is ready to send even his own son to death, though ultimately dissuaded by the people (14:43–45). In many ways he strikes me as not bad, but admirable.

On the other hand, Saul is far from faultless. I have already argued that he appears inept in chapter 9 when he and a servant are out looking for his father's lost animals: it is the servant who must suggest they seek out a "man of God" (who will turn out to be Samuel), and, when Saul wonders what to use for pay, it is again the servant who provides the answer. In short, the leadership qualities Saul shows on the battlefield are not always with him in domestic matters. The pattern continues in the next chapter as the Israelites search for the newly chosen king: he is hiding among the baggage (10:22), showing a domestic fearfulness inconsistent with his battlefield behavior.

Or is it inconsistent? A second look at the military Saul reveals flaws there too. The oath by which the king forbids his people to eat until the battle is over (14:24) can be seen as foolish; Jonathon, in fact, says as much (vv. 29–30). More important, Saul seems careless in fouling up the letter of God's command to destroy all the Amalekites in chapter 15. (I want to return to this incident shortly.) He fears Goliath (17:11), a cowardice emphasized by young David's success against the giant. He becomes insanely jealous of David (18:7–9), turning to everything from attempts to spear him to the wall to wild-goose pursuits across the countryside. And throughout his career, Saul has a mind easily turned by others. We have already seen how he is instructed by his servant and dissuaded from killing Jonathon by the people. In chapter 19, he agrees to Jonathon's request that he cease his attempts to kill David (vv. 4–7), but moments later tries pinning him to the wall again (vv. 9–10). Later still he will twice humble himself before David's chiding (24:16–21; 26:21, 25), yet even David realizes his words cannot be trusted (27:1). Some of this, of course, is a sign of Saul's developing madness, but the pattern of inconsistency, of acceding to whoever has his ear—and then often reverting—is there from early on.

So Saul is neither a monster of vice nor a paragon of virtue; he has strengths, but considerable weaknesses, too. It might be possible to fear for him in the Aristotelian sense, yet those weaknesses loom large to me. They seem not minor flaws but pervasive defects. Keep this in mind as we proceed to the question of pity. Is Saul's suffering more than he deserves? I must admit real doubt as to whether he is treated fairly by Samuel—or even by Yahweh. At one point he is cursed for offering a sacrifice to the Lord when Samuel (who had instructed the king to wait seven days for *him* to make the offering) doesn't show up as promised (13:11–14; cf. 10:8). At several later places "an evil spirit from the Lord" afflicts Saul (for example, 16:14), and near the end, neither God nor Samuel will answer his inquiries about what to do before the final Philistine attack (28:6, 16)—a marked contrast to the Lord's constant answers to David's calls for help, even when David is traitorously serving the Philistines (for example, 30:8).

On the other hand, there is evidence that what happens to Saul results from one or more instances of his own hamartia—unfortunate decisions that rebound upon him. The decision to offer the sacrifice without Samuel is ambiguous, but—more fateful still—in chapter 15 he does not kill the Amalekite king and the best of his animals, despite the Lord's order to "not spare them, but kill both man and woman, infant and suckling, ox and sheep, camel and ass" (v. 3). Both instances show a touch of pride—almost a Greek hubris—in Saul, who takes matters into his own hands rather than fully accede to his prophet or his God. And both result in Samuel's declaration that the Lord will desert Saul because of them (13:13–14; 15:22–23).

Still, I must confess to a feeling that, all things considered, Saul is more sinned against than sinning. I feel for him. Yet when I put the questions of fear and pity back together, I'm reminded of those pervasive defects. Perhaps what I feel for Saul is not pity for a tragic hero, but sympathy for a pathetic victim.

Which leads to the third question: does Saul's fall result, in part at least, from his own strengths? He himself cites leadership—an acknowledged strength—as his explanation for offering the sacrifice, telling Samuel, "When I saw that the people were scattering from me, and that you did not come within the days appointed, and that the Philistines had mustered at Michmash, I said 'Now the Philistines will come down upon me at Gilgal, and I have not entreated the favor of the Lord'; so I forced myself, and offered the burnt offering" (13:11–12). Yet I have argued that Saul's leadership is tainted by his tendency to listen to whoever now has his ear, and here he implicitly blames "the people," in "scattering" from him, for his choice. Is his decision, then, an act of strength or weakness?

The issue is clearer in chapter 15, where he is told to punish the Amalekites for their hindrance of Israel on the Exodus, sparing no one. At first I am tempted to credit Saul for restraint—another acknowledged strength—in sparing the king and the best of the animals (he seems less vicious than the Lord himself), and to accept his explanation that the animals were spared only to be sacrificed to the Lord (v. 15)—that is, that they would be destroyed, though ritually. And the Lord's orders had not specifically mentioned the king, though they did instruct Saul to "utterly destroy all that [the Amalekites] have . . . [and] kill both man and woman . . ." (v. 3). But alas, Saul himself reveals that his motives are not restraint and sacrifice, but his lifelong tendency to be persuaded by those at hand. He first tries to hide his guilt by implicitly separating his acts from the people's: "*They* have brought them [the animals] from the Amalekites; for *the people* spared the best of the sheep and of the oxen . . . and the rest *we* have utterly destroyed" (v. 15)—but eventually, makes full confession to Samuel: "I have sinned; for I have transgressed the commandment of the Lord and your words, *be-*

cause I feared the people and obeyed their voice" (v. 24). Pathetically, he grabs and tears Samuel's robe at the prophet's words of rejection (v. 27). Again, a fateful choice that might have tragically come from strength is tainted by weakness.

What does cause Saul's fall, it seems to me, is not his strength, but his weakness—combined with an external circumstance. That circumstance is his rejection by the Lord, which leads him to disturbing behavior and degeneration either directly—his two attempts to pin David to the wall are preceded by visits from the Lord's evil spirit (18:10–11; 19:9–10)—or indirectly—he summons the medium of Endor only after the Lord refuses to answer his inquiries (28:6–7). I sympathize with Saul here, for God's rejection seems based on technicalities, on petty failures to obey the letter of instructions; it is as if God has turned on Saul (whom he chose in the first place, remember) to show the Israelites that his early misgivings about a king (see 8:7–9) were justified. Yet Saul's petty failures derive from his weakness. Moreover, not all his "madness" can be traced clearly to the Lord. In chapter 22 he orders eighty-five priests killed because he thinks (wrongly) they have conspired with David, and he does so, not through an evil spirit from the Lord, nor through rejection, but through his own jealousy— an acknowledged weakness. This jealousy, coupled with ineptness (another weakness), leads him to follow David all over the wilderness in a mad attempt to capture and kill him; he is no more successful finding David than he had been with his father's animals. Like most tragic heroes, Saul is a victim of forces beyond his control, but unlike the best, his problems result more from weakness than from strength.

What remains is to test how Saul stands up to the last of my criteria for the tragic hero: how does he meet his fate when doom is upon him? Again I find ambiguity, but this time in a different direction. When told by the ghost of Samuel that he and his sons will die in battle, Saul is so scared he falls "at once full length upon the ground" (28:20); in short, this man who began his career vertically "from his shoulders upward . . . taller than any of the people" (9:2) winds up horizontally flat on the earth. Yet next day he musters the courage to enter the fray despite knowing his fate; he will no longer "hide among the baggage." When the battle goes badly he takes his own life—a cop-out, it might seem, yet he falls on his sword to preserve honor ("lest these uncircumcised come and thrust me through, and make sport of me" [31:4]), and only after his armor-bearer refuses to kill him. The battle ended, Saul's body is mutilated by the Philistines in a final disgrace—yet the people of Jabesh-Gilead retrieve it and the bodies of his sons for proper burial. Ambiguity, yes, but I can't help feeling that Saul has attained a nobler stature at the end than ever before, that almost nothing becomes his life like the leaving it, for what strikes me about the final chapter is not weakness but strength, not fear but honor.

Then what of the bottom line? I think Saul is a mixed bag as tragic hero. His fortune moves from happiness to misery, yet his happiness is clouded by confusion, and his misery may be his finest hour. He has the strengths and weaknesses to elicit fear for "the man like ourselves," yet his weaknesses are considerably pronounced. His suffering seems undeserved enough to elicit pity, yet even his unfortunate choices seem motivated by weakness; indeed, his degeneration and fall stem more from weakness than from strength. Only at the end does the balance seem to shift: despite ambiguities, he meets his fate squarely and stoically. Perhaps Saul's greatest "tragedy" is that he falls just short of being a tragic hero; he is a little bit Hamlet, and a little bit everyman.

But no matter what literary label we apply to this story, it is one that presents us with a perplexing vision of the human predicament. Here is a man, with strengths as well as faults, chosen by a power much larger than himself for a role that had never before existed—a role that may be too big for him. Here is a man who confronts ambiguous choices (what would *anyone* do if the seven days were up and Samuel had not appeared to offer the sacrifice as he had indicated?) and who makes unfortunate decisions that lead to his downfall. Here is a man whose degeneration seems brought about by factors both within and beyond his control. Finally, here is a man who can muster the strength to pick himself up from the floor at Endor and stoically meet the death he knows is inevitable. The story of Saul presents a view of life I cannot fail to ponder.

VI

David:
A Study in Politics

*(1 Samuel 16–31; 2 Samuel 1–24;
1 Kings 1:1–2:12)*

Every four years we in the United States experience the political ritual of a presidential campaign. And we know in advance that the outcome will depend in no small part on who has made the wisest moves at each stage of the game. The successful candidate, for example, often collects political IOUs by stumping for local nominees, perhaps years before his own campaign begins. He is also very careful to time his formal announcement properly: if he enters the fray too soon, he may lose momentum, and if too late, he may never pick it up. We also know that certain kinds of events are likely to derail even a front-runner: how often has a leading candidate been irreparably damaged by the sudden revelation of scandal in his family or personal life?

The story of David provides a fascinating study in such politics. Begin by examining our first encounter with him in 1 Sam. 16. He is only a boy, out tending the sheep, as the prophet Samuel comes to anoint one member of his family as new king of Israel, even while Saul still holds the throne. Samuel is convinced that an older brother of David's will be the Lord's chosen and almost overlooks the lad, until God makes it clear that David is the one he has in mind. "Then Samuel took the horn of oil, and anointed him in the midst of his brothers, and the Spirit of the Lord came mightily upon David from that day forward" (v. 13). It is an intriguing little story, yet one of its implications can be easily overlooked: almost from the moment we first meet him, David *knows* that he is the Lord's chosen, that he has already been anointed king. There is a kind of inevitability about his career that he must be aware of from the start. I think the story of that career must be read against this fact.

With this in mind, examine David's slow but steady rise to prominence from 1 Sam. 16 to 2 Sam. 5. Notice how, like many politicians, he rises from obscurity. When we first meet him he is the youngest son of Jesse, almost omitted, as we have seen, from the parade of sons Samuel reviews—yet he is the one whom the Lord has chosen. Immediately thereafter we learn that Saul is seized by an evil spirit, and David, heretofore unknown at court, is brought in to soothe the tormented king. Within a few verses, Saul comes to love him dearly, and he becomes the king's armor-bearer (1 Sam. 16:14-23). In the very next chapter, Goliath rears his frightening head, and soon a little-known young man, who had wandered to the battle site almost by accident, is felling him with a slingshot. In rapid succession we encounter three instances that reveal David as a nobody with obvious potential to become a somebody. And his origin has scores of parallels: how many recent American presidents—to continue that analogy—have risen to the top from obscure middle-class backgrounds?

Consider other aspects of David's rise to power. For example, he eclipses the present leader. In the later chapters of 1 Samuel, though Saul is king, David is clearly on the move, in control of the situation. It is he who takes the offensive, roaming about with Saul madly chasing him here and there. He is the political new kid on the block, the rising star whom the king recognizes as a real threat. The repeated chant "Saul has slain his thousands, and David his ten thousands" (for example, 1 Sam. 18:7) suggests that the people also see what is happening: David's star is on the rise even as Saul's declines.

Notice next how David establishes key friendships that will be of use to him later. Jonathon, of course, is his liaison with Saul's court. Whatever else might be said about this relationship, it is of immense help to David, who uses it even to know when to flee for his life (1 Sam. 20). Later, in exile, David will win the friendship of many who are "in distress," becoming a kind of guerrilla leader over them (1 Sam. 22:1–2); clearly these people will be indebted to him. He establishes strategic ties, then, to those with power and to those without it, winning early assistance and support from within the royal family and from among the masses. Much like a presidential candidate stumping for other office-seekers and identifying himself with popular causes, he paves the road for future success.

But David knows the value of caution as well. Like many a politician, he bides his time, refusing to grab power too quickly. I see a hint of this in his early reluctance to use Saul's armor in fighting Goliath: "I cannot go with these," he tells the king, "for I am not used to them" (1 Sam. 17:39). He is speaking of his personal discomfort and awkwardness, to be sure, but also, I am convinced, of the inappropriateness of his assuming the trappings of kingship at this early stage. The same discretion will cause him to twice hold back from slaying Saul, though he has the chance, once while Saul relieves himself in a cave (1 Sam. 24), and again while the king sleeps surrounded by his army (1 Sam. 26). "Who can put forth his hand against the Lord's anointed, and be guiltless?" he asks (1 Sam. 26:9), and then, remembering that he himself has been anointed by Samuel and need only wait to assume the throne, adds "As the Lord lives, the Lord will smite him; or his day shall come to die; or he shall go down into battle and perish" (v. 10). Again like the politician who knows the importance of timing in announcing her candidacy and making her moves, David holds back lest he upset the necessary chain of events.

But holding back is not the same as total passivity, as David shows in his ability to outmaneuver his opponents. Immediately following Saul's death, most of Israel turns to Saul's son Ishbosheth as their new king. But David has already been anointed king by the men of Judah at Hebron, thus making a strategic inroad on his competitor (2 Sam. 2:3–4; cf. vv. 8–10). Soon his forces will defeat those of Ishbosheth and his commander, Abner (vv. 29–32). Indeed, when Ishbosheth is killed, Abner begins to switch allegiance to David and promises to "bring over all Israel," suggesting the new king's ability to draw others, though they be opportunists, to himself (2 Sam. 3:12–16; note how David can now give orders to Abner, demanding that his former wife Michal be returned to him before any negotiations take place; clearly, he is bargaining from strength). In the midst of all this, a generalizing statement in the text underscores all that is happening: "David grew stronger, while the house of Saul became weaker and weaker" (2 Sam. 3:1). Whether by strategic inroads and military victories of his own, or switched allegiances of others, David can successfully outmaneuver his competitors, as any politician must do.

Finally, notice David's ability to create, or at least capitalize on, "fortunate occurrences." When Joab kills Abner in an act of personal revenge, David is quick to remove himself from blame (2 Sam. 3:26–30). Yet it has to be to his ultimate advantage that this associate of Saul, turncoat or not, be removed! This leads to an intriguing question: is David, despite his protests, responsible for the killing? On the one hand, his righteous anger against Joab certainly seems extreme: "I and my kingdom are forever guiltless before the Lord for the blood of Abner the son of Ner. May it fall upon the head of Joab, and upon all his father's house; and may the house of Joab never be without one who has a discharge, or who is leprous, or who holds a spindle, or who is slain by the sword, or who lacks bread" (vv. 28–29). Yet, when all is said and done, Joab remains, not only alive, but commander of David's army (compare 8:16)! May we paraphrase Prince Hamlet's mother to say of David, "Methinks the king doth protest too much"? If so, if he is even indirectly responsible for Abner's death, then he is indeed a master of political deceit.

But even if David is innocent of this bloodshed, the incident still shows his uncanny ability to *use* luck, to benefit from the turn of events. Several other key enemies will be dispatched like Abner— among them, Saul (see the alternate account of his death in 2 Sam. 1:1–16), and Ishbosheth (2 Sam. 4:5–12)—and each time David will unequivocally distance himself from the killing, even to the point of executing the killers. I think the text is tantalizingly ambiguous about David's role and sincerity in all this, but regardless, his career is advanced and strengthened by each death. Whether David is calling the shots, whether the Lord is overseeing events, or whether things are "just happening," David is the ultimate benefactor. Again like many politicians, he either creates or benefits from luck.

Thus several factors characterize David's rise to power: his emergence from obscurity, his eclipsing the present leader, his establishing key friendships, his biding his time, his outmaneuvering opponents, his ability to make use of luck. They are factors that explain the rise of many a leader. In David's case, they leave him at the height of his power: king over both Judah and Israel (2 Sam. 5:3–5). And it is now, with virtually all the Israelites behind him, that he executes a master stroke. To choose a capital in Judah would alienate some northerners; to choose one in Israel would alienate the south. So David chooses Jerusalem—a non-Israelite town on the border between north and south (2 Sam. 5:6–10). It is a move akin to the choice of Washington, D.C.—neither a northern nor a southern city, but a new metropolis carved from both territories—as the capital of the United States. In short, David is good at his profession; he knows how to rise to the top and, it would seem, how to stay there.

But staying there will not be easy. For, as so often happens, David is so intent on his professional life that he gets careless with personal and domestic affairs, and these will prove his undoing. Though he is never permanently unseated, the remaining years of his life will be marred by problems and mistakes that represent a clear falling off from his earlier success.

There is a hint of this in 2 Sam. 6. David dances uninhibitedly while the Ark of the Lord is brought into Jerusalem, angering his wife Michal, Saul's daughter, who complains that he has behaved like "one of the vulgar fellows" (v. 20). David quickly retorts, "it was before the Lord, who chose *me* above *your* father, and above all *his* house, to appoint *me* as prince over Israel . . ." (v. 21). In short, his political triumphs, perhaps gone to his head, bring out old family jealousies. The incident is soon over (though we are told in verse 23: "Michal the daughter of Saul had no child to the day of her death"), but it is a harbinger of things to come. David's professional career will become increasingly intertwined with his personal life, largely to his dismay.

The real turning point comes in 2 Sam. 11, in the affair with Bathsheba. There is an ominous hint in the first verse: "In the spring of the year, the time when kings go forth to battle, David sent Joab, and his servants with him, and all Israel; and they ravaged the Ammonites, and besieged Rabbah. But David remained at Jerusalem." At a time when kings have a customary duty in the field, in other words, David stays home and delegates the job to another. He is becoming lax in his duties. And he will come to regret this laxity, for while he is home, he spies Bathsheba bathing on a neighboring rooftop.

The affair quickly snowballs, David becoming guilty of greater and greater misconduct. He sends for the woman—the wife of Uriah the Hittite, who is fighting for David in the field—and has interourse with her, before her purification, thus committing adultery and violating ancient law (v. 4). Almost immediately she sends word that she is pregnant, and David frantically tries to cover his sin by recalling Uriah from battle, buying him off with a gift, and insisting that the husband return to his own house—"to wash his feet" (v. 8), of course. But Uriah is adamant; he will not go to his house, eat, drink—or lie with his wife—while his comrades are camped in the open field. Desperate, David sends a message, through Uriah, to Joab, ordering that Uriah be placed "in the forefront of the hardest fighting . . . that he may be struck down and die" (v. 15). And when this happens as planned, David can add deceit and murder to his list of wrongdoings.

In short, the king's behavior is not simply bad, it is awful. And it is hardly undercut by his blindness to the point of Nathan's parable in the next chapter, a blindness the prophet must pierce through with his dramatic "*You* are the man" (12:7). God himself will not stand for this; as Nathan observes, "Thus says the Lord, 'Behold, I will raise up evil against you out of your own house'" (12:11). And that is exactly what happens.

In rapid succession, a series of family scandals leads David on a downhill slide. His daughter Tamar is raped by her half-brother Amnon (2 Sam. 13). This in turn leads another of David's sons, Absalom, to avenge his sister by killing Amnon (vv. 28–29). Yet terrible as incest and fratricide may be, these events do not bother David nearly so much as his next major problem: the rebellion of Absalom. For here, the impingement of a personal crisis on David's professional life will be made most dramatically clear.

What may make this crisis especially difficult for David is the number of ways Absalom resembles his father. We are told, for example, of his striking good looks: "Now in all Israel there was no one so much to be praised for his beauty as Absalom; from the sole of his foot to the crown of his head there was no blemish in him" (14:25).

Physical descriptions are rare in the Bible, which is perhaps why this detail recalls for me what we were told earlier about the youthful David: "Now he was ruddy, and had beautiful eyes, and was handsome" (1 Sam. 16:12). But there is more. Following the murder of Amnon, Absalom is for a time banished from his king—as David lived a fugitive from Saul. Absalom slyly gathers supporters for himself from among the discontented of the land (2 Sam. 15:2–6)—as David did in the cave of Adullam (1 Sam. 22:1–2). Absalom plans to have himself proclaimed king in Hebron (2 Sam. 15:10)—the same city in which David first wore the royal crown (2 Sam. 2:1–4). And while David is forced into exile from Jerusalem, Absalom sleeps on the rooftop with his father's concubines (2 Sam. 16:21–22), repaying David for his indiscretion with Bathsheba (compare 2 Sam. 12:11–12, where the Lord had predicted such a consequence for David's sin).

In short, while watching Absalom, David sees his own life pass before him, and so despite the political consequences of the conspiracy, retains great feeling for the boy. He gives orders to "deal gently for my sake with the young man Absalom" (2 Sam. 18:5), and when, nonetheless, the rebel is killed, lapses into a poignant lament: "O my son Absalom, my son, my son Absalom! Would I had died instead of you, O Absalom, my son, my son!" (18:33). His grief is so intense that he must force himself to return to public duty, following Joab's rebuke (19:1–8). Nowhere else in his story does the conflict between public and private, between professional and personal, so strongly afflict the king of Israel.

Thus personal and domestic troubles begin to take their toll on David's political life. And to be sure, we now find the king making professional mistakes, too. In 2 Sam. 24, for example, he angrily orders a census of Israel and Judah, then repents of his decision and seeks the Lord's forgiveness by setting up an altar. The incident is clouded by the fact that it is the Lord who inspires the census (v. 1) and by ambiguity over why such an act should be considered evil, but the bottom line seems clear: David has done something inappropriate in his administration of the kingdom. The man who made every right move in his rise to the top is now fouling up.

So David's fall is precipitated by personal misconduct and furthered by family scandal, open rebellion, and professional mistakes. As if these weren't enough, to them is now added the inevitable results of aging. There are hints of this problem in 2 Sam. 21:15–17, where the heretofore tireless king grows weary in battle and almost loses his life, but for me the most poignant revelation of David's aging is at the very beginning of 1 Kings. "Now King David was old, and advanced in years," we are told, "and although they covered him with clothes, he could not get warm" (1:1). A beautiful maiden is brought in to minister to him, "but the king knew her not" (v. 4), that is, had no intercourse with her. The implication seems clear: he didn't, because he couldn't—yet another sign of the debilitation and humiliation of age.

Yet pathetic as physical aging is, the final irony is a sign of mental aging, or senility. David, the master politician, is now outfoxed by Nathan into naming a successor. Though David has said nothing about who shall succeed him, his eldest surviving son, Adonijah, assumes it will be himself and begins preparations for his investiture (1 Kings 1:5–8). But Nathan prefers Solomon, a son far from the eldest and hardly a prime candidate. The prophet tells Bathsheba, Solomon's mother, "Go in at once to King David and say to him, 'Did you not, my lord the king, swear to your maidservant, saying "Solomon your son shall reign after me, and he shall sit upon my throne"?'" (v. 13). Now when has David ever made such a promise? But as the king listens to Bathsheba, and then to Nathan, who furthers his plot by entering the king's presence at the right moment and supplementing her words, he seems reminded of something that never happened and says to Bathsheba, "As I swore to you by the Lord, the God of Israel, saying 'Solomon your son shall reign after me, and he shall sit upon my throne in my stead'; even so will I do this day" (v. 30). His senility played upon, David now becomes a victim, not a perpetrator, of political maneuvering.

The story of David is a classic case study of a political career. As we have seen, his rise is marked by a combination of factors that have brought many to power; and his fall, by factors that have brought many to ruin. Yet almost always he remains the master politician. Nowhere do I see this more clearly than in his final instructions to Solomon (1 Kings 2:5–9), containing understated but clear advice on what to do with David's enemies and friends. Not only does the advice reveal his sense of justice; it more clearly suggests his powers of discretion, indirection, manipulation, and deceit. For the man who can say, for example, of Shimei, "I swore to him by the Lord, saying, 'I will not put you to death with the sword,'" and immediately add to Solomon, "Now therefore hold him not guiltless, for you are a wise man; you will know what you ought to do to him, and *you* shall bring his gray head down with blood to Sheol" (vv. 8–9), is a man capable of both the best and the worst in politics.

Throughout the centuries David has been called many things, including king, psalmist, founder of the messianic line. But few such labels are more appropriate than "classic politician." In his rise and in his fall, he provides us with a fascinating and insightful study indeed.

VII

Elijah and Ahab: Another Portrait of Divinity

(1 Kings 17–22; 2 Kings 1–2)

In an earlier chapter we examined the Flood story for some of its implications about a view of the biblical God. Many have suggested that if the Bible is literature, this God is its central character. It is therefore appropriate to return to this question again, to see what the stories of Elijah the prophet and Ahab the king add to this portrait of Yahweh, the Lord God of Israel, and, by extension, what they imply about the evolving biblical concept of divinity.

First, however, I want to emphasize an important point about portraits. A friend once recollected a time when she was asked by her kindergarten teacher to draw a picture of her family. She produced the usual stick figures for herself, her sister, and her father—but drew her mother with huge circles for head, torso, and extremities, laughingly adding that her mother was not an exceptionally large person and that the drawing may have reflected a psychological truth—a mother's imposing presence in the life of a small child—more than any physical reality.

Her point, I think, has wider ramifications. Pictures are always far removed from the things they claim to depict. Even the finest portraits, the most realistic photographs, are but images of their subjects, impressions of limited moments in time that reflect at best partial truths about "the real world." Many, in fact, reveal as much about their artist's momentary perceptions of that world—witness my friend and her mother—as anything else. And so a lifelike picture of a smiling man dressed in a business suit tells us little of what he is like when frowning or when dressed casually at home; indeed, it provides only a glimpse of what he may be like on a good business day. The image is not the thing.

This is important to bear in mind when considering the Bible, a book filled with word-portraits about subjects both human and divine. Is the David we considered in the last chapter the "real" David? In one sense, yes: the biblical material is our primary source of information about him. But in another sense, no: what we examined was a narrative presenting a portrait of David, subject to the same limitations affecting all portraits. The issue is even more significant—and more complex—when we consider a word-portrait of God: to what extent are we speaking of the "real" God? Clearly we are now on the boundaries of religious faith, and all readers must answer this question for themselves. But bear in mind that I am talking here about a *portrait* of the Lord as he appears in just one portion of the Bible—indeed, about *my* reading of that portrait–and that portraits are limited perspectives on their subjects.

With that in mind, let's return to the question at hand. You will recall my arriving at several conclusions about the God of the Flood story: he is very powerful; he practices retributive justice (though his quality of mercy is ambiguous); he is a loving parent, but one who can relate to his children through covenants; he is awesome, though not without anthropomorphic qualities; he is more flexible than unchanging. What will we now find about the God who works within the lives of Elijah and Ahab?

For one thing, I am again impressed by his great power, though this time not so much by its depth as by its breadth. Indeed, the depth of that power—though always great—seems somewhat undercut by the way it is revealed through a human intermediary; in the Flood narrative, the Lord had worked directly, while here—though he is clearly the source of power—he usually works through his prophet. But he works in a way that reveals power to do many things, with human life, with the natural world, and with competing gods.

He has, for example, the ability to sustain life. Twice in 1 Kings 17 Elijah is mysteriously fed, first by ravens, then by the widow of Sidon, though she barely has enough for herself and her son. Clearly in these instances, the food that sustains life comes from the miraculous intervention of the divine. But the Lord also shows that he can not only sustain life, but restore it. When the widow's son appears to die, Elijah calls upon his God, "and the Lord hearkened

48

to the voice of Elijah; and the soul of the child came into him again, and he revived" (v. 22). Admittedly there is an ambiguity, since the text does not say the boy was dead but that "there was no breath left in him" (v. 17)—but the bottom line is that we are shown a very powerful God with immense influence over life.

The Lord's power is not limited to human life, however; he can also control nature. This is seen in his pervasive influence over rain (for example, 1 Kings 17:1 and 18:1), but more dramatically in 2 Kings 2 as first Elijah, and then his successor Elisha, perform the Lord's "favorite miracle," the parting of the waters (this time of the river Jordan; see vv. 8 and 14). Thus the breadth of his power is vast: he can sustain life, restore it, and control the natural world.

There is an irony in all this, however, since throughout this narrative, the Lord is in competition with the Canaanite god, Baal (note Elijah's ultimatum at 1 Kings 18:21). Baal is a god of fertility and nature, who should have special authority over life and water. Yet it is Yahweh, the Israelite God, who performs the life-sustaining and restoring miracles, who controls the water and the rain. And this irony is brought to the fore in the dramatic confrontation that makes clear yet another dimension of the Lord's power: his ability to defeat a competing god.

When Elijah recognizes that many Israelites are turning to Baal, he challenges the prophets of this god to a contest. He and they will each prepare a sacrifice and invoke their respective deities to miraculously ignite it. Despite the exhaustive efforts of Baal's prophets (1 Kings 18:26–29), their god does not respond. Then Elijah adds to the drama by dousing his sacrifice with water, making it virtually impossible to ignite. (The situation is not unlike those laundry commercials where Brand A is tested against Brand X, with the shirt Brand A must wash deliberately made extra dirty to show its greater strength.) Yet light it the Lord does; his fire "fell, and consumed the burnt offering, and the wood, and the stones, and the dust, and licked up the water that was in the trench" (v. 38). The power of the God of Israel is no match for the god of Canaan; it is a power over things both on earth and in the heavens.

What about other qualities in this portrait of Yahweh? In the Flood story, the Lord struck me as clearly concerned with retributive justice, rewarding the righteous and punishing the wicked. I find the same concern here, on scales both large and small. On the large scale, he is ready to destroy those who have turned away from him to other gods, though this time he will work through human avengers instead of a flood (1 Kings 19:17). Similarly, he is willing to save the remnant that has remained faithful, saying to Elijah, "Yet I will leave seven thousand in Israel, all the knees that have not bowed to Baal, and every mouth that has not kissed him" (v. 18).

On a smaller, more personal scale, the Lord evidences the same kind of justice in the incident of Naboth's vineyard. Ahab, acting like a spoiled adolescent, moans and groans because Naboth will not sell his vineyard, which the king wants for a vegetable garden (1 Kings 21:1–4). Then Ahab's wife, Jezebel, intercedes, essentially "putting out a contract" on Naboth, whose death allows the king to claim the land (vv. 8–16). But the Lord will stand for none of this; he instructs Elijah to tell Ahab: "Have you killed, and also taken possession? . . . In the place where dogs licked up the blood of Naboth shall dogs lick your own blood" (v. 19). Later he issues a similar edict against Jezebel (v. 23). Misbehavior is met with immediate threat of punishment.

This time, however the Lord *seems* to show a clearer sign of mercy than he had in the Flood story. God had also threatened destruction for Ahab's house (vv. 21–24), but when the king responds to Elijah's words with repentance, the Lord relents, telling Elijah, "Have you seen how Ahab has humbled himself before me? Because he has humbled himself before me, I will not bring the evil in his days; but in his son's days I will bring the evil upon his house" (v. 19). Again, however, I find this "mercy" perplexing. For one thing, the treatment of Ahab's son seems neither merciful nor just. More important, God's decision seems of little avail to the repentant Ahab, who will indeed be killed as originally promised (22:37–38)—and, as we shall see, through a devious trick instituted by the Lord!—and whose dynasty will still eventually fall. In short, divine mercy once again seems more apparent than real.

What about the Lord's relationship to his people? In the Flood story I argued that while he might be termed a loving parent, he tended to relate to his "children" in covenantal terms. Here, I am most struck by the way he demands strict obedience. We have seen this tendency before: Moses gets into trouble for lack of such obedience (Num. 20), for example, and so does Saul (1 Sam. 15). In this story, note how an unnamed prophet is attacked by a lion because he refuses to strike another prophet as the Lord has commanded (1 Kings 20:35–36). Later, the Lord is angry when Ahab fails to kill the king of Syria, whom the Lord has "put under a ban" (that is, commanded to be destroyed as an act of religious devotion): "Because you have let go out of your hand the man whom I had devoted to destruction, therefore your life shall go for his life, and your people for his people" (20:42; God says this before promising Ahab the mercy mentioned earlier). There is no room for wavering here; the Lord expects strict obedience from his people, and their failure to supply it is met with retaliation.

What about the nature of this God himself? In the Flood story, we saw a God who was awesome, yet not without humanizing traits. I find the same paradox here, though once again with the emphasis on the less anthropomorphic, more ineffable quality of the divine. So the Lord will speak with Elijah, as one person might with another, yet in the next breath will perform a dramatic miracle emphasizing his distance, his divine otherness. Again, as Elijah hides in a cave, the Lord can "pass by," as a person might pass by one's house, but he is hardly tangible, seeming to appear, not even in the wind, earthquake, or fire that accompany his passing, but in a mysterious "still small voice" (1 Kings 19:11–13). This is a God impossible to pin down, a God of opposites who both has human qualities and transcends them, who can rend mountains and yet be heard as a quiet voice.

A surprising element in the Flood story was the Lord's flexibility. Nothing in the Elijah/Ahab episodes contradicts that, but one element suggests to me a quite different perspective: this God seems inescapable. In 1 Kings 22, Ahab, about to join the king of Judah in a battle to reclaim Ramoth-gilead, is afraid because of the dire prediction of Micaiah. (We will return to that strange prophecy in a moment.) Asked about the advisability of the battle, Micaiah replies, "I saw all Israel scattered upon the mountains, as sheep that have no shepherd; and the Lord said, 'These have no master; let each return to his home in peace'" (v. 17). Apparently afraid for his life, Ahab decides that he will disguise himself in battle but that his ally Jehoshaphat, king of Judah, should wear the royal robes (v. 30). His intent is clear: the enemy, not realizing he is a king, may divert their attention to Jehoshaphat, and Ahab will avoid becoming the missing shepherd the Lord's prediction has referred to. But disguises will not thwart the Lord's purpose; we are told "A certain man drew his bow at a venture, and struck the king of Israel . . ." (v. 34). Not only does Ahab die, but his army is scattered like the "sheep" the Lord had referred to (v. 36), and his blood is licked by dogs, as the Lord had also foretold (v. 38). This God is indeed inescapable; despite Ahab's machinations, every word spoken by the Lord is fulfilled.

So further insights or different perspectives are suggested here about the Lord's power, justice, mercy, relationship to people, nature, and flexibility. Does this portrait of divinity pick up on any things not stressed or not included in the Flood portrait? I think two examples will show that the answer is "yes" on both counts.

Something not stressed in the Flood story was the Lord's presence. Tradition tells us the biblical God is omnipresent, is somehow everywhere at once. Perhaps that notion is taken for granted in a narrative about a divinity whose flood destroys nearly all his creation and who always seems available when needed. But the Elijah/Ahab narrative makes a point of stressing that the Lord is at least not a localized God; he has a wider domain than some think. When Ahab's forces defeat Benhadad, king of Syria, in 1 Kings 20, the Syrians argue that this has happened because the Israelite gods are "gods of the hills"; were the battle waged on the plain, they surmise, surely the Syrians would win (v. 23). Assuming the Lord has geographical limits, Benhadad attacks on the plain. Yet even though the Israelites are "like two little flocks of goats" before the Syrian forces, they defeat the stronger power, and a prophet tells Ahab why: "Thus says the Lord, 'Because the Syrians have said, "The Lord is a god of the hills but he is not a god of the valleys," therefore I will give all this great multitude into your hands, and you shall know that I am the Lord'" (v. 28). The incident clearly

suggests the Lord is not a localized deity, is not as
as some would suspect, an element perhaps impli
phasized, in the Flood narrative.

What about an insight not included at all in the rlood story?
There is at least one, and it is missing not only from Gen. 6–9 but
from most traditional assumptions about the biblical God. An intriguing incident in the Elijah/Ahab material suggests the Lord is
not above deception.

In 1 Kings 22 the prophet Micaiah, asked why his prediction of
the outcome of the proposed war with Syria differs from that of
other prophets, replies: "I saw the Lord sitting on his throne, and
all the host of heaven standing beside him on his right hand and
on his left; and the Lord said, 'Who will entice Ahab, that he may
go up and fall at Ramoth-gilead?' And one said one thing, and
another said another. Then a spirit came forward and stood before
the Lord, saying, 'I will entice him.' And the Lord said to him, 'By
what means?' And he said, 'I will go forth, and will be a lying spirit
in the mouth of all his prophets.' And he said, 'You are to entice
him, and you shall succeed; go forth and do so.' Now therefore
behold, the Lord has put a lying spirit in the mouth of all these
your prophets; the Lord has spoken evil concerning you" (vv. 19–
23).

The point is self-explanatory: the Lord can authorize, can indeed
instigate, entrapment and deception. This strange notion may be
partially explained by a seldom-recognized fact: the Hebrew Bible—the Old Testament—does not reflect clear belief in a conventional devil who can be blamed for evil. The serpent who tempts
the woman in the Garden of Eden is not identified in Genesis as a
devil. Even the Satan who appears in the Book of Job is less an
embodiment of evil and more an assigned opponent (*satan* in Hebrew means "adversary"), a kind of devil's advocate. In the absence
of a traditional devil, evil must eventually be traced to God. And
so, as we have seen, it is the Lord who attempts to kill the Moses
who is doing his bidding (Exod. 4:24–26), who sends an evil spirit
upon Saul (1 Sam. 16:14), who incites David to institute the census
for which the king must then repent (2 Sam. 24:1; cf. 1 Chron.
21:1, where a later narrator retells this incident and blames Satan

instead of the Lord). The account of the lying spirit fits this context.

But the context should not obscure the point: the Lord is deliberately entrapping and deceiving Ahab—the very king to whom he has just promised mercy (21:29). This is indeed a warts-and-all portrait of divinity, and it suggests that the biblical God will sometimes employ—to say the least—unorthodox tactics.

We are far from a complete analysis of the Bible's portrait of Yahweh. But we have seen enough to recognize, I think, that that portrait is evolving. This narrative reinforces and expands on some points introduced in the Flood story, showing us a God whose power is broad as well as deep, whose concern with justice is clear (though his mercy remains ambiguous), whose authority demands strict obedience, whose nature is paradoxically both like and unlike that of humans. It introduces a new angle over and above that of Gen. 6–9, revealing a deity whose flexibility is here de-emphasized in favor of his being inescapable. It picks up on a point only hinted at in the Flood story—that God's domain is not limited by locale—and introduces a notion not found there at all: that God can authorize entrapment and deception. Whether this represents a change in the deity or a people's evolving understanding of their God is an important question to be considered elsewhere. But it gives us a great deal to think about as we consider our own concept of divinity.

A portrait, as I said earlier, is not its subject. It is an impression of that subject caught in a fleeting moment, a reflection, at best, of partial truths. But portraits give us cause to stop and meditate, and that which we have investigated in the Elijah/Ahab narrative is no exception. As you reread this narrative, and the others that comprise the Bible, you can fill in more brushstrokes of the book's "central character," and use these to further refine your understanding of the biblical God.

VIII

Jonah:
Two Problems with Thinking

(Jonah 1–4)

Living in the great age of computers, we strive for clear, unbiased, analytical thinking. Yet this goal remains more an ideal than a reality. Much thinking is still marked by unintended and unrecognized weakness. Two common problems are illustrated in the following incidents.

Incident one: several years ago some friends and I were discussing "our most disillusioning moments." As the conversation went on, one friend (a historian) surprised us by saying he had been quite disillusioned as a young man when he learned George Washington had false teeth. At the time this sounded trivial indeed, but I think he was getting at this: we have a tendency to glorify our heroes so much that we often forget their humanity. By placing them on pedestals, we unconsciously practice prejudicial thinking: we "prejudge" such people before considering all the evidence, acknowledging (indeed, often exaggerating) their accomplishments, while ignoring their weaknesses, their false teeth.

Incident two: a while back, a television network conducted a survey with ten questions, including this one: "An accused murderer is brought to trial and found innocent. After his acquittal, he openly admits he was in fact guilty. Should he be brought to trial again?" Almost everyone responded, "Yes." At the bottom of the survey, beneath the tenth question, was this additional query: "Do you support the American Bill of Rights?" Again, nearly everyone answered in the affirmative. The results clearly showed an unconscious contradiction between the responses to questions one through ten (each question, while not mentioning the Bill of Rights, involved a situation covered by them), and the response to the final question. The Bill of Rights is, of course, the first series of amendments to our Constitution, designed to protect individuals

55

from the government. Trying an acquitted person a second time for the same crime is a direct violation of the Fifth Amendment—even if the person is guilty. The respondents were displaying divided thinking—they had separated their thoughts into compartments so they could accept the Bill of Rights on an abstract level without realizing that on another level they were not willing to follow through on its implications.

Prejudicial thinking and divided thinking are parts of the human nature we all share. I think the Book of Jonah sharpens our insights on them through two interwoven examples of a literary device not often recognized in the Bible: satire. The first makes a point about the prophets themselves—and ultimately about prejudicial thinking surrounding many heroes. To see how it works, I want to suggest three clues for detecting light satire in this kind of narrative.

First, audience familiarity with the satire's object. To recognize any satire, we have to know the phenomena in the "real world" being satirized. A take-off on television news broadcasts means nothing if we have never seen the 11:00 news. If the Book of Jonah pokes fun at the prophets, therefore, we must expect its audience to be aware of "real prophets"—Elijah, for example, and the writers found among the Latter Prophets. But certainly no reader of the Bible, ancient or modern, can lack such awareness, at least in a general sense.

Next, the satire's similarity to reality. Narrative satires must resemble their real-world objects enough so the audience catches the connection; thus a TV news send-up will generally include an anchorperson, several other reporters, special segments for weather and sports, and news stories that sound, at least at first, as though they could be real.

Notice how the Book of Jonah resembles other prophetic books. For one thing, it uses traditional language: "The word of the Lord came to Jonah son of Amittai" (1:1; compare 1 Kings 17:2). In the Hebrew Bible, it is placed among the Latter Prophets. The character Jonah, though never called a prophet, has a clear prophetic mission: to convey the word of the Lord to a people. And Jonah even has strange idiosyncracies, like Elijah or Ezekiel; how many people do you know who have spent three day and three nights in the belly of a great fish?

So far, nothing I've said distinguishes Jonah from any other prophetic book. But now for the third and final clue: the satire's alterations of reality. Narrative satire must change and exaggerate the real world just enough to let us know straight seriousness is not intended. So the anchorperson in a satire may speak in a squeaky voice, and his reports turn out to be off the wall. Such alterations are the "kicker": the clear sign that we as audience have a right to cry "satire!"

Where do I find them in the Book of Jonah? First, examine the book's form: unlike other works among the Latter Prophets, which are mostly in verse, Jonah is primarily written as a third-person prose narrative, an inconclusive yet clear signal that something unusual is going on here. Second, note the people to whom Jonah is sent: not Israelites, but their great enemy, the Ninevites. (Nineveh was the capital of the Assyrian Empire, which had destroyed the Northern Kingdom of Israel and frequently threatened Judah.) Next, observe how Jonah lacks the acquiescence of other prophets: told to go to Nineveh, he flees instead in the opposite direction, to Tarshish. (Contrast Elijah's reaction to God's instructions in 1 Kings 17:3ff.)

Then there is the question of success. While other prophets struggle incessantly to bring a wavering people back to the Lord (again, compare Elijah), Jonah speaks *one* line—"Yet forty days, and Nineveh shall be overthrown!" (3:4)—and immediately the whole city repents, including the king (a traditional antagonist to a prophet) and the animals. In fact, Jonah "converts" another whole group of people without even trying, when the Gentile sailors pray and sacrifice to the Lord while throwing Jonah overboard (1:14–16). He has the most amazing success record in prophetic history! Given that, I would expect to find him gratified, if not exhilarated by his accomplishments. Instead, just the opposite: he is bitter and angry as he prays at the beginning of chapter 4.

What is the purpose of all this? Perhaps the satire is gently reminding us that, whatever else they may be, prophets are human beings, too. In so doing, it may make a point about prejudicial thinking; despite our tendency to glorify such heroes, they have warts and foibles—false teeth, if you like. If the book was written, as many scholars think, in the fourth century B.C.E., when the great age of prophecy had passed, it could be suggesting a revisionist view of prophets, reminding us that we sometimes need to distinguish their will from the divine will, to refocus our image of them. In a broader sense, it may make a point about human attitudes toward not only prophets, but also other heroes, serving as a corrective lens toward the dangers of prejudicial thinking.

But interwoven with this idea I find another bit of satire that makes a more profound point. It has to do with Jonah's struggle to comprehend fully the nature of his God, a struggle that leads him unconsciously into divided thinking.

In chapter 1, as the sailors try to determine why they have been beset by such violent storms, they seek out Jonah and ask, "And whence do you come? What is your country? And of what people are you?" (1:8). The twice-repeated question is a strong clue that something important is about to be said. Jonah answers, "I am a Hebrew, and I fear the Lord the God of heaven, who made the sea and the dry land" (1:9). He is a worshiper, not of any god, but of Yahweh, whom he knows to be a creating, universal God, responsible for everything; he "made the sea and the dry land." Later, Jonah will reveal something else he knows about Yahweh: he is "a gracious God and merciful, slow to anger, and abounding in steadfast love, [who] repentest of evil" (4:2). On an intellectual level, Jonah understands the Lord quite well. His descriptions are traditional biblical fare (besides Gen. 1–2, see Exod. 34:6–7); they represent the "realistic" element in this satire.

It is on the practical level that Jonah runs into problems, and I see these through the satire's "alterations." Notice Jonah's psalmlike prayer in chapter 2. It is full of subtle ironies, but one thing should be immediately clear: it posits a God concerned exclusively with *one* person—*not* the universal God who made both sea and land: "*I* called to the Lord, out of *my* distress, and he answered *me*; out of the belly of Sheol *I* cried, and thou didst hear *my* voice" (2:2). It is true that many psalms take this personal stance, and yet interesting that the same Jonah who has just declared his God to be universal, now utters a prayer emphasizing a very personal, even self-centered, relationship to that God.

This evidence alone is far from compelling. But there is more. When told to preach to Nineveh, for example, Jonah flees in the opposite direction. On one level, he knows his God is universal, yet on another, he acts as though he can escape from God's presence. Later, when the Ninevites repent and God cancels the doom Jonah had predicted, the prophet is downright bitter (4:1). On one level, he knows his God is not only universal but compassionate, yet on another, he is unable to accept a practical implication: how can God be solicitous toward Israel's *enemy?* Somehow, this kind of compassion challenges Jonah's sense of divine integrity, and he says "I pray thee, Lord, is not this what I said when I was yet in my country? That is why I made haste to flee to Tarshish. . . . Therefore now, O Lord, take my life from me, I beseech thee, for it is better for me to die than to live" (4:2,3).

Divine universality and compassion are fine as ideas, but when practiced in this way they seem to Jonah inconsistent with divine justice: Israel's enemy should be punished, not forgiven. And in a sense, he is right, just as a patriotic American is rightly offended when an acquitted person acknowledges his crime, yet legally escapes punishment. But this reading reminds me that higher values sometimes lead to practical problems. And since Jonah's difficulty is not with God in theory but with God in practice, the book appropriately ends with the Lord delivering to his prophet the very practical lesson of the plant that springs up and then withers, at the end of which he drives home his point: "You pity the plant, for which you did not labor. . . . And should not I pity Nineveh, that great city, in which there are more than a hundred and twenty thousand persons who do not know their right hand from their left, and also much cattle?" (4:10–11).

In its own time, the Book of Jonah may have addressed the relationship between Jews and other peoples, its satire arguing subtly yet strongly that the isolationism favored by many in the establishment was inconsistent with traditional teachings about the Lord. In our era, it still reminds me of the dangers of divided thinking, a human weakness all too easy to slip into.

I find enough clues in the text of this narrative to indicate a satiric thrust. That satire suggests to me a pattern concerning human thinking. In emphasizing the dangers of both prejudicial and divided thinking, it steps out of its place in history to speak to us all, as great literature always does.

IX

Psalm 23:
The Maturing of Faith

It goes without saying that the Bible is a religious book that deals with religious issues. One such issue is faith. Here is a word we toss around rather loosely, however. What is faith? How does it develop and grow?

Both questions have several possible answers. To the first, we might respond that faith means belief in ideas that lack rational proof, like the articles of a creed. In another sense, it may mean trust, as in the expression "I have faith in God as a good leader." Or it may describe an orientation, an attitude toward the world— perhaps one that says the glass is not half-empty, but half-full. The philosopher Paul Tillich defined faith as "the state of being ultimately concerned," the condition of giving oneself over to whatever promises total fulfillment, the object of such faith being anything from a deity to love, power, or money. In this latter sense, at least, faith seems a "universal" phenomenon: while its objects may differ, most everyone may have it.

Suppose we were to zero in on the second definition: faith as trust. How does such faith develop and grow? Again, there are several possibilities. It may grow through experience, as one learns that the person or thing that is the object of faith has deserved and earned the trust. It may be strengthened by community: seeing where and how others place their faith can encourage us to do likewise. Or it may mature through a crisis or period of hardship: if faith has helped us through such a problem, it can be stronger when the difficulty passes.

All of which brings us to Psalm 23. Here is a poem many know by heart (usually in the King James Version). Here is a poem that has been turned to countless times as a piece of inspiration, a source of consolation, even as a funeral hymn. And—though it is not always so recognized—here is a poem that may tell us something about the nature and development of faith.

But before we consider such matters, I want to address a problem. Psalm 23 is a poem—a kind of literature with which most of us are uncomfortable. The most familiar kind of literature to us is prose narrative: we feel more at home, I suspect, in the world of the novel or short story. Rarely do we read poetry, especially short lyric poetry, unless forced by a cruel and inhumane English teacher! And when we must submit, we often try to read the poem as though it *were* prose fiction. We look for characters and find few, for a plot and find none. Sometimes we can't even discover conventional sentences. Little wonder that many give up in despair.

I think there is a way around this problem, a method for reading poetry that is simple, yet different from that we would use for a novel. It involves four steps, each of which I will introduce and apply to Psalm 23. At the end, we can see what the experience has helped us learn about the maturing of faith.

Here is Psalm 23 as it appears in the Revised Standard Version.

The Lord is my shepherd, I shall not want;   1
    he makes me lie down in green pastures.   2
He leads me beside still waters;
    he restores my soul.   3
He leads me in paths of righteousness
    for his name's sake.

Even though I walk through the valley of the   4
      shadow of death,
   I fear no evil;
for thou art with me;
    thy rod and thy staff,
    they comfort me.

Thou preparest a table before me   5
    in the presence of my enemies;
thou anointest my head with oil,
    my cup overflows.

> Surely goodness and mercy shall follow me   6
>   all the days of my life;
> and I shall dwell in the house of the Lord
>   for ever.

Step one is to read the poem through the first time for vocabulary and dramatic situation. Vocabulary is especially important in lyric poetry, a highly concentrated form of literature in which each word is charged with meaning. While most of the language in this psalm seems straightforward enough, I find at least two words worth checking, either in footnotes or in a good Bible dictionary. The *rod* of verse 4 seems to have been a stout cudgel about three feet long, often used to ward off predatory animals, while the *staff* was a longer pole, possibly with a hook at one end, sometimes used to guide timid sheep over difficult terrain. In other words, together these tools provide protection, discipline, and guidance. Such information will prove useful in a moment.

Dramatic situation refers to facts we can ascertain about the speaker, audience, time, or location of the poem. Sometimes that information is precious little. The "I" of verse 1 tells me this speaker is a single person, for example, but other than that, he—or she—is not identified. (Whether or not the psalm was written by David, as tradition has it, the speaker—as a "created" narrator—could be just about anyone. In fact, for simplicity, and to emphasize the psalm's universality, I'll use female pronouns from here on.) Note that the psalm does not call the speaker a shepherd, by the way; it is the Lord who is so labeled. Regarding audience, notice that in verse 1 the Lord is referred to in the third person, perhaps suggesting the speaker is talking to someone else—a third party, or herself— about God. The third person continues through verses 2 and 3, but, surprisingly, in 4 and 5 the speaker switches to *second* person: "for *thou* art with me. . . ." And just as strangely, in verse 6 she goes back to third: "the house of *the Lord*. . . ." Perhaps she is addressing a third party in verses 1–3, switching to a prayerlike direct address to God in 4–5, and back to the third party in verse 6. In any case, to me she seems in more straightforward contact with the Lord in verses 4–5 than in either the beginning or the end of the poem. We will have to wait a moment to ask why. For now, let me finish off dramatic situation by observing that I don't find in the psalm many clues as to time or place: the words could be uttered almost anytime, anywhere.

Step two in this reading process asks us to record our first impressions of the poem. This refers to both value judgments (do I like the poem or not?) and ideas (what do I think the poem is about?). The first time I analyzed this poem in this translation I remember being mildly surprised by its variations from the so familiar King James language ("my cup overflows" instead of "my cup runneth over," for example). But I recall liking the poem because it seemed "pleasant." As for ideas, my first guess was that the speaker was trying to express the comfort and consolation that the Lord represents for her. I was convinced Psalm 23 was a comforting, yet simple, little poem.

Step three invites us to return to the beginning of the poem for a closer look, a second reading in which we examine it line by line, word by word. I find it interesting that this psalm begins with "the Lord"—in the Hebrew Bible, the personal name of the deity, suggesting greater intimacy than the more formal and distant "God." Notice too that this Lord inspires confidence; trusting in him, the speaker "shall not want." But now observe that the Lord is metaphorically called "my shepherd"—suggesting, of course, that the speaker is a sheep, an animal traditionally thought of as innocent, trusting, and dumb. Play around for a moment with the implications of this shepherd-sheep relationship. A keeper and his animal are not simply master and servant; they are members of two different species. The gap that separates them is not of degree, but kind. Thus I find an interesting tension: despite the intimate note in the name "Lord" and the clear sense of trust implied here, the speaker seems to sense a wide gulf between God and herself at the beginning of the psalm.

I think this notion is reinforced in verses 2–3 as we learn that the Lord/shepherd is the active one, doing all the work ("*he* makes me lie down. . . / *He* leads me. . . / *he* restores my soul / *He* leads me. . . / for his name's sake"), while the speaker/sheep is completely passive. The first time the speaker refers to a self-initiated action is in verse 4 (the RSV emphasizes this shift with a break in the text between 3 and 4)—and it is an action that bodes ill: "Even though I walk through the valley of the shadow of death. . . ." (Notice, by the way, that the trouble is not necessarily death, but something unspecified that is *like* death; the Hebrew suggests "valley of deep darkness.") This first mention of trouble is followed by the shift to second-person pronouns: "for *thou* art with me; / *thy* rod and *thy* staff, they comfort me." The speaker's problem, in other words, leads to a closer, more personal relationship with the Lord. She is consoled by his presence, by the protection, discipline, and guidance provided by his shepherd's tools. Moreover, throughout verses 1-4, she trusts the Lord as a provider of needs—though interestingly, mostly *physical* needs for the here and now, from pastures to lie down in to the rod and staff that comfort. (Even the "soul" and "paths of righteousness" of verse 3 can be translated, respectively, "life" and "right paths," indicating physical phenomena desired for the present.)

The second person continues as we move to verse 5, but something else has changed: the nature of the images. In verses 1-4 we had an extended sheep metaphor, with references to green pastures, still waters, a rod and a staff—parts of a sheep's world. Now we are told of a table being prepared, a head anointed with oil (a sign of special favor, used, for example, in proclaiming a new king), a cup being filled. The images have become human. (Again the RSV reinforces the shift with a break between 4 and 5.) In short, I find the speaker's self-image improved. She now sees herself as a person, not an animal—still inferior to the Lord, but of a higher order. She is growing up.

I think this new attitude carries over into the psalm's final verse, where the speaker expresses confidence that she will be provided with spiritual needs ("goodness and mercy") in the future, not only the immediate physical needs of the earlier verses. The trouble past, she reverts to the third person in the final part of verse 6 while stating unequivocally that she will now play an active role: "*I* shall dwell in the house of the Lord / for ever." Whether this last word denotes "eternity" or—as most scholars now suggest—"my whole life long," confidence remains, but gone is the passivity of the opening verses, that might have rendered this thought "the Lord will lead me into his house." The speaker's understanding of the Lord, and of herself, has matured.

But where is the message about faith? For this we must turn to step four of the reading process, a step that asks us to reconsider our initial impressions—about both evaluation and ideas—from step two. Then I said I liked this psalm because it seemed "pleasant"; I thought it was about comfort and consolation. Now, after a careful analysis, I find myself more impressed by the profundity of the poem. It touches on many human issues, including awareness of God, the self—and faith. For Psalm 23 seems to me to be talking about faith as trust: notice the strong note of confidence in the Lord from beginning to end. In its few verses, I find a growth in that faith, from the simple, sheeplike passivity of the opening lines to the more mature, human involvement at the end. And what seems to have led to this growth are two things: a *crisis,* a brush with trouble, a walk through "the valley of the shadow of death," and also a kind of *experience:* having come through this trouble with the help of the Lord, the speaker has learned that her trust was well placed. She sees her God in a new light, realizing that as she matures she can continue to depend on him for spiritual gifts like goodness and mercy, as well as physical needs. She also sees herself in a new light, recognizing that she can participate actively in the divine-human relationship.

In short, the psalm has confirmed several of my earlier suspicions about faith and its growth—that faith is trust, that it can develop through crises and experience. But it has reminded me of other things, too, including the notion that the maturing of faith can bring with it a changed attitude toward one's God and one's self. Far from being a naive, simple little poem, Psalm 23 provides profound insights about important dimensions of the human condition.

X

Job:
The Problem of Suffering

(Job 1–42)

A young man stops on a dark deserted highway to help a stranded motorist with a flat tire. While he works on the car, another driver, unable to see clearly, accidently runs him over, making him a paraplegic for life.

A young girl is attacked by a brutally sadistic rapist. She is molested, strangled, left for dead. But she survives, and the nightmare haunts her from then on. The rapist is never apprehended.

A hurricane destroys the towns and villages of a small Asian country. Six thousand are killed, thousands more left homeless and starving. Among the survivors are orphaned infants and children, three years old and under.

The problem of human suffering is as much with us now as in the days when Job was written. It remains one of the most perplexing and profound of questions, especially in the context of the Bible, where it assumes the form of an issue philosophers call *the problem of theodicy:* how can a good and powerful God allow such things to happen? Perhaps we can investigate what a reading of the Book of Job suggests about its nature, causes, and consequences.

First, a brief note about the nature of Job's suffering. It seems to me this man's affliction assumes several forms, almost simultaneously. He suffers materially, losing his vast possessions; personally, being deprived of his children and alienated from his wife (2:9–10); physically, enduring "loathsome sores"; socially, having to deal with the "helpful advice" of friends; psychologically, experiencing the anguish reflected in his long poetic speeches. His case reminds me that the most intense suffering is rarely monolithic: the paraplegic and rape victim of my opening examples receive more than physical scars, the hurricane survivors, more than material losses.

But a more important question is, *why* does Job suffer? Let's begin with Job himself. In the opening chapters, we are told explicitly that he is a "blameless and upright" man, both by the narrator (1:1) and by God (1:8). Even after his afflictions, he does not turn to sin (1:21–22; 2:10–11). Except for a possible tinge of scrupulosity or self-righteousness when he offers sacrifices for his children, fearing *they* may have sinned (1:5)—and even this can be seen as further evidence of his piety—it seems to me that Job is completely innocent and good, that his suffering is *not* a punishment for sin. In this respect, the Book of Job runs counter to some notions I find elsewhere in the Hebrew Bible—in the Garden of Eden, for example, where the sufferings imposed on the serpent, woman, and man seem clearly retributions for behavior, or in Judges, where the Israelites' fate depends on how closely they have adhered to, or wavered from, the word of the Lord.

If the fault lies not in Job, how about Satan? For us, his name and reputation make him a natural candidate for responsibility. But this is not yet the Satan of later Jewish and Christian tradition; as I suggested in discussing the Elijah-Ahab narrative, the modern concept of the devil is largely foreign to the Hebrew Bible. So in Job 1–2 (he does not reappear later in the book) Satan seems a member of the Lord's heavenly council (he is found among "the sons of God" [1:6])—not an outcast from heaven like the Satan of the New Testament. He is not so much divine enemy as adversary (the meaning of his name in Hebrew), countering God as a kind of "devil's advocate" who argues that Job's righteousness stems only from his having everything he could wish for (1:9–11; 2:4–5).

Satan does, to be sure, serve at least two traditional "devil" functions: he both tempts and afflicts—but with important twists. He tempts Job to curse God—though not through enticement, like the Eden serpent, but through its opposite—and twice afflicts the man—always, however, with express permission and within clearly defined limits (1:12; 2:6). If he is responsible for Job's suffering, he strikes me as more an immediate than an ultimate cause.

Which leads inevitably to the third major figure of the opening chapters: God himself. What is his role in Job's suffering? Some have suggested that God here appears as a self-satisfied potentate, bragging to his council about his outstanding servant (1:8). Whether this is true or not, two things are certain: it is God who first brings up Job's name (is he tempting Satan?), and it is he who grants permission for, and sets limits to, Satan's work.

Why does God allow this suffering? Is it to test Job's faithfulness? His conversations with Satan imply this possibility. "Put forth thy hand now and touch all that he has, and he will curse thee to thy face," predicts Satan (1:11), and God agrees to the trial. Is it to win a bet? His deal with Satan does assume the form of a wager, God bragging of his servant's righteousness, Satan challenging, "I'll bet the guy won't be so good if you let me heap a few afflictions on him," and God responding, "You're on." Is there any good reason? After the first round of afflictions has left Job's integrity intact, God claims Satan "moved me against him, to destroy him *without cause*" (2:3). Perhaps it is all three factors at once; perhaps the suffering results from a test that becomes a wager that God then realizes is foolish. Yet immediately after noting Job has suffered "without cause," the Lord allows Satan to try again (2:6)! It is as if Job is a victim of divine whimsy.

God will have more to say about all this, though Job will have to wait a while to hear it. But we can take a quantum leap to Chapter 38, where God speaks out of the whirlwind, and return later to the important intervening chapters. In chapters 38–41, the Lord speaks twice to Job, and what he says has been the subject of endless debate. Here are several interpretations to consider in light of the three possible divine motives—a test, a wager, no good reason—I found in chapters 1–2:

—*Might makes right.* In this view, the Lord intimidates Job with his power and grandeur ("Where were you when I laid the foundation of the earth?"). This seems petty, yet there is little doubt that in the biblical context, God speaks with justification. He *was* there at the beginning; Job was not. He *does* control the natural world; Job does not.
—*Divine freedom.* In this view, God resists Job's attempts to box

him in, to force him to be good to Job because the man has behaved well. In his acts and later questioning, Job may be trying to manipulate the Lord, implying "I've done my part in being good; now you must do yours in providing reward." Is God saying Job has no right to expect such an iron-clad bargain, to impinge on divine freedom and inscrutability? Is this behind his question at 40:8: "Will you even put me in the wrong? / Will you condemn me that *you* may be justified?" If so, is he denying—or at least superseding—the concept of retributive justice, wherein the good are rewarded and only the wicked punished?

—*Limited divine power.* In his book *When Bad Things Happen to Good People*, Rabbi Harold Kushner suggests an intriguing possibility: that God is not *all*-powerful, that he cannot prevent *all* suffering, *all* "pockets of chaos" in the universe. Kushner sees God saying, "Though it may not be perfect, I made the best world I could. Can you make a better one?" He sees Job's vision of God changing from that of a powerful figure who causes suffering to that of a loving figure who shares his creature's grief. Before dismissing this possibility, understand that the divine name usually rendered "Almighty" (as in 40:2) is *Shaddai*, which literally means (according to some scholars) "the one of the mountains"—hardly suggesting omnipotence. On the other hand, is Kushner's implication that God could not have prevented Job's suffering consistent with the opening chapters of the book?

—*Limited divine goodness.* The other side of Kushner's coin must also be examined. If God *is* powerful enough to prevent Job's afflictions, are we to conclude from this book that he is not all-good? After all, it might be argued, he allows Job to be tormented to win a bet, then pulls rank to shut off his complaints. Are there signs of divine love and goodness in the Lord's speeches, or anywhere else in the book?

—*Limited human perspective.* In this view God emphasizes his greater perspective, which allows him to see in a different light what Job may consider unjust. The two-year-old caught playing innocently with matches on the kitchen floor may scream with indignation when his playthings are abruptly taken away, seeing nothing but injustice, while the parent views the same event as an act of concern and love. Is this what God has in mind when he asks "Shall a faultfinder contend with Shaddai?"—with the perspective of "the one of the mountains" (40:2)?

—*Unknowable answer.* This view approaches the problem from the negative by stressing that in his speeches God does not indicate why Job suffers. He does not say it is a test, or a wager, or anything else; neither does he deny such possibilities. The implication, then, is that humans will not, perhaps cannot, know the reason. The issue is clouded for me, however, by discrepancies between what I find in chapters 1–2, where we are, as it were, eavesdropping on the divine council, and what I find in chapters 38–41, where we get God's public explanation, an account lacking any reference to his opening conversations with Satan. It is like hearing the White House tapes, then receiving the president's official pronouncement. Is there a sense in which God is covering up the real explanation?

One thing seems clear: the Book of Job does not provide simple, straightforward answers to what causes suffering. It does present a righteous man who does not seem a victim of punishment, yet who suffers immeasureably in many ways. It does present a Satan who tempts and afflicts, but whose efforts are strictly controlled, suggesting him as an immediate, not an ultimate, cause. And it does present a God who appears in command, yet whose motives are difficult to pin down, the possibilities ranging from a test of faithfulness to a divine cover-up. Perhaps they are right who say the book does a good job of posing the problem of theodicy, but does not answer it.

If it is hard to determine exactly what the Book of Job suggests about causes of suffering, perhaps we will have better luck examining consequences. How does Job change throughout his ordeal? In many ways his lengthy dialogues in the middle chapters resemble a grieving process such as we might go through following the death of a loved one. Yet, though Job has lost his children, I don't think it is them he grieves for. He hardly mentions them. Nor does he talk much about his lost possessions or even his loathsome sores. What he really mourns for, I think, is something less tangible—his belief, derived from his culture's tradition, that his righteousness should protect him from suffering. It is the loss of this notion—that good behavior merits a clear reward from the Lord—that seems hardest for him to bear. He constantly asks to be shown where he has gone wrong, constantly pleads for the chance to bring his case before an impartial arbiter. If he had sinned, at least he could fall back on the comforting and understandable doctrine that affliction is his punishment. But he knows he is innocent and so much give up that time-honored belief.

Notice the movement of Job's attitudes following the afflictions, as he struggles to retain his sense of divine justice. Initially, he seems to acquiesce, accepting what has happened as an example of God's prerogative: "Naked I came from my mother's womb, and naked shall I return; the Lord gave, and the Lord has taken away; blessed be the name of the Lord" (1:21; cf. 2:10). Then his three friends Eliphaz, Bildad, and Zophar, come and sit with him without speaking for seven days, providing Job with company, silence, and time (2:13). Finally the shock of the afflictions wearing off and reflection settling in, Job himself breaks the silence. Cursing the day of his birth, he turns to self-pity and yearns for death:

> Why is light given to him that is in misery,
>   and life to the bitter in soul,
> who long for death, but it comes not,
>   and dig for it more than for hid treasures;
> who rejoice exceedingly,
>   and are glad when they find the grave?   (3:20–22)

At this point Job must begin to deal with the advice and "help" of his friends. Earlier, his wife had offered her blunt suggestion—"Curse God, and die"—but that was before the passage of time had allowed him to reflect on the matter, and he had quickly dismissed her (2:9–10). The words of the friends will be longer and, at least initially, less direct, yet they will keep circling back to this position: somehow, Job is being punished for his guilt. (Compare, for example, Eliphaz at 4:7–9, Bildad at 8:20, Zophar at 11:4–6.)

This is, after all, the message of retributive justice so ingrained in their tradition. Even the younger Elihu, though he claims to speak differently (32:14), mouths the same sentiments (34:10–11).

But Job, though acknowledging this conventional wisdom in theory, cannot see how it applies to his case (6:24). Observe carefully his anguished responses to the friends. Not only do they resemble an emotional grieving process (the loss of his concept of rewards and punishments is hard to bear), they also lack logical progression, not to mention the proverbial "patience of Job." In true-to-life fashion, Job jumps around, repeats himself, even contradicts himself, much as the friends are doing. He moves back and forth, it seems to me, among complaint (for example, 6:15–17), bitterness (7:11), despair (9:22), frustration (9:32–33), sarcasm (12:1–2), alienation (13:24–26), fear (13:20–21), castigation (14:1–3), hope (16:19), loss of hope (17:1), nostalgia (29:1–6), and throughout, persistent proclamations of innocence (6:30; 12:4; 27:5–6; 31:1–40).

And then, the voice from the whirlwind, and Job's submission—a double submission, at that, made after each of God's speeches (40:3–5; 42:1–6). How should we take it? Is Job, having worked through the grief process, now ready to acquiesce, to give up the notion that virtue protects one from suffering? (If so, he has come full-circle, since his first reaction in the opening chapters was a kind of acquiescence.) Is he, though not satisfied, unable to do anything but submit in the face of God's immense power? Or is there another explanation?

Perhaps there are clues in the ways Job changes after his submission. He is, to be sure, restored to the world: his possessions are doubled (42:10), his place in society renewed (v. 11), another family provided (v. 13). The last years of his long life seem happy ones. But more important, Job is restored to his God. He has learned something about, and grown closer to, the Lord. "I had heard of thee by the hearing of the ear," he says, "but now my eye sees thee" (42:5). He had known God indirectly, through the tradition espoused by his friends—a tradition accepted theoretically by Job, though he refused to apply it to his own situation—but now he has encountered him straight on, through experience. And this new relationship is reciprocal: not only does Job feel closer to God, but God seems closer to him. Whereas Job's prayers for his children in chapter 1 failed to prevent their destruction, his prayers for the friends in chapter 42 are heeded (v. 9). Perhaps Job submits, then, because at last he has what—though he did not know it—he has wanted all along: a more direct relationship with his God.

Most intriguingly, though, Job seems to me vindicated by the Lord, who tells Eliphaz "My wrath is kindled against you and against your two friends; for you have not spoken of me what is right, *as my servant Job has*" (42:7; essentially repeated in v. 8). I have always wondered how to take that comment. Is God implying that suffering is *not* a punishment for sin—the position repeatedly proclaimed by the friends? If so, there *is* one definite notion about what causes suffering in Job: it is not retribution for behavior. Or is God saying Job is right to struggle with his suffering instead of piously mouthing traditional sentiments? If so, perhaps the Book of Job tells us that, whatever its causes, suffering—if endured steadfastly and questioned earnestly, if worked through as a kind of grieving process—can have positive results, bringing restoration to one's world and one's God.

Reading the Book of Job has its problems, and we can certainly argue about the meaning of a passage, the nature of the message, even the literary integrity of the whole. But few can deny the grip it has had on us for over two thousand years. In addressing the problem of suffering, in getting us to think about its nature, causes, and consequences, it demonstrates perhaps like nothing else the power with which the Bible can speak to the human condition.

XI

Ruth:
A Study in
Interpersonal Relationships

(Ruth 1–4)

A subtle sign of our personality is how we relate to others. There are times, I suspect, when each of us is very selfless, showing real concern for another person; other times, when we wallow in self-pity. There are times when we see others as full human beings, practicing a relationship Martin Buber called "I-Thou"; other times, when we see them as objects to be manipulated for our own ends—what Buber called "I-It." There are times when our motives for relating to others are noble and virtuous; other times, when they are despicably self-serving. And we have seen people illustrate both extremes and middle ranges of these spectrums.

Reading the Book of Ruth may sharpen our insights about interpersonal relationships. To investigate, I want to focus on five characters—the unnamed "next-of-kin," and then Orpah (Ruth's sister-in-law), Naomi, Boaz, and Ruth—and ask four questions about each: What kinds of relationship does each engage in? (I will use the tendency to fall short of, meet, or exceed "expectations"—what law or common courtesy require—as touchstone.) To what extent does each manipulate another? What motivates each to relate to others? Is each consistent in the way he or she relates, or do changes and developments occur?

Let's begin near the story's end, with the next-of-kin. In his brief appearance, what kind of relationship does he practice? Israelite law commanded a nearest relative to redeem the property of an impoverished kinsman (Lev. 25:25). Furthermore, a deceased's brother was expected to marry his widowed sister-in-law and produce children to carry on the dead man's name (Deut. 25:5–6). Technically, neither law applies in this case, for the impoverished kins*man*—Naomi's husband Elimelech—is dead, and the next-of-kin is not brother-in-law to Ruth. Still, the assembled elders seem to accept Boaz's implication that the man's duty—or at least his right—remains. He quickly shows he is willing to meet expectations if no complications arise: he will redeem Naomi's land (4:4). But when marrying Ruth is thrown into the bargain, he backs off (vv. 5–6), removing his sandal (v. 8)—the very sign used in Deut. 25:8–10 to embarass a brother-in-law who refuses his duty. In short, I think he relates to others by ultimately falling short of expectations: he will perform a simple duty, but not one that pushes him too far.

What about the other questions? Does he practice manipulation? It seems to me he does, though of course on a small scale. He treats Naomi, Ruth, and Boaz as *things* (compare Buber's I-It): he will use them if to his advantage, otherwise turn them aside. His motives, though not fully developed, boil down, I think, to self-interest: he offers to redeem the land either for its value or to retain his honor before the assembled elders, but refuses Ruth lest he "impair [his] own inheritance" (4:6)—that is, confuse the distribution of his own estate. Finally, he reveals at least an outward change regarding relationships: he quickly moves from willingness to perform one duty, to rejection of another. All told, though he is hardly evil—commentators have observed there are no villains in this story—I think he relates to others weakly, falling short of expectations, manipulating, acting from self-interest, and developing in a negative direction.

Let's move from him to Orpah, another figure with a brief role, this time near the story's beginning. In contrast to the next-of-kin, Orpah relates to another by going beyond expectations—though only so far. Her husband, brother-in-law, and father-in-law dead, she accompanies Naomi on the road to Bethlehem, something the older woman implies is not necessary, since Orpah has already met her obligations with kindness (1:8–9). With Ruth, she refuses her mother-in-law's first attempt to send her back (v. 10). But Naomi's second plea is enough, and after it Orpah kisses the older woman and returns to her own land (vv. 14–15). In so doing she shows me a degree of manipulation: though not as callous as the next-of-kin, she, too, eventually turns from Naomi when the woman is of no more use to her. (Naomi has just argued that she cannot bear more husbands for her daughters-in-law.) Moreover, her motive again seems self-interest: ultimately, she will look out for herself in her own country. And like the next-of-kin, she demonstrates a quick but dramatic change in a negative direction, from accompanying another to taking care of herself. Again she is hardly evil, and overall I think she relates better than the next-of-kin, but when pressed, she quickly falls aside.

From two minor characters, we come now to Naomi, a more complex figure, to be sure. At first, it seems to me, she neither falls short of nor exceeds expectations; she simply does her duty, urging her daughters-in-law to look out for themselves and acceding only reluctantly to Ruth's persistence (1:15–18). Yet later, she goes beyond expectations in helping Ruth find a mate (3:1). I don't think her motives are purely altruistic, but before we examine them, look at how Naomi, too, manipulates others. When Ruth announces she has been gleaning in the fields of Boaz, a light turns on in the older woman's mind. "The man is a relative of ours," she exclaims, "one of our nearest kin" (2:20). Immediately she sizes up the situation and, subtly but firmly, begins to orchestrate the match. She starts innocently, telling Ruth, "It is well, my daughter, that you go out with *his* maidens, lest in another field you be molested" (v. 22), but soon is giving explicit instructions (3:1–5). She tells Ruth both what to do—"Wash therefore and anoint yourself, and put on your best clothes"—and what *not* to do—"do not make yourself known to the man until he has finished eating and drinking"; later, when Ruth reports what has happened, she again counsels restraint: "Wait, my daughter, until you learn how the matter turns out, for the man will not rest, but will settle the matter today" (3:18). In short, she cagily sets up both Ruth and Boaz; like a skillful chess player, she moves her figure (Ruth) to "influence" her opponent (Boaz), knowing when to act and when to wait. She is not a callous manipulator; her concern for Ruth, and for Boaz, though mingled, as I shall argue, with self-interest, seems real. Yet she manipulates all the same, reminding me that not every instance of "using" others is undesirable.

So Naomi at one point meets her obligations and at another exceeds them, practicing her own brand of manipulation. What about her motives? As I've already hinted, these too seem mixed. In chapter 1 she dismisses her daughters-in-law out of apparent concern for their welfare: "Go, return each of you to her mother's house. May the Lord deal kindly with you, as you have dealt with the dead and with me" (v. 8). But this concern either masks or is mingled with her own bereavement, as the end of her second speech shows: "No, my daughters, for it is exceedingly bitter to me for your sake that the hand of the Lord has gone forth against me" (v. 13). Later, she expresses concern for Ruth—"My daughter, should I not seek a home for you, that it may be well with you?" (3:1)—but only after learning of the girl's meeting with Boaz, the kinsman whom Naomi quickly sees as the means of her own salvation too. For in providing a family for Ruth she will provide one for herself, restoring, as it were, the offspring she has lost. Indeed, near the end the women of Bethlehem proclaim that Naomi now has a daughter-in-law better than seven sons, and the old woman takes her "grandchild," lays him in *her* bosom, and becomes his nurse, leading the neighbors to observe "A son has been born *to Naomi*" (4:15–17). In this woman, altruism and self-interest mix in a healthy combination.

Which leads to a final note about Naomi: like the next-of-kin and Orpah, she too changes in her relationship to others, but her development is more extensive and, though less straightforward, ultimately positive. She begins with concern for her daughters-in-law that hides or accompanies her own anguish, but soon withdraws into self-pity; returning to Bethlehem she tells the towns-women, "Do not call me Naomi [Hebrew for 'pleasant'], call me Mara ['bitter'], for the Almighty has dealt very bitterly with me. I went away full, and the Lord has brought me back empty. Why call me Naomi, when the Lord has afflicted me and the Almighty has brought calamity upon me?" (1:20–21). Later, this gives way to a moment of revelation as Naomi sees in Ruth's meeting with Boaz a sign that the Lord *has* kept faith after all: "Blessed be he by the Lord, whose kindness has not forsaken the living or the dead!" (2:20). Moving out of self-pity, she begins to orchestrate the match, concerned for Ruth and for her own welfare, and winds up fulfilled and praised by the women, her family restored. In short, I think she passes from a sorrowful concern/bereavement, through self-pity, to an awakened faith, then to a more healthy concern/self-interest. Her development is extensive, its outcome good.

And that takes us to Boaz, a man who, more clearly than others, relates to another by going beyond expectations. Finding Ruth in his field, he immediately singles her out for special instructions (2:8–9). Later he allows her to go beyond normal limits in gleaning; Israelite law allowed the poor to take what was left in a field after reapers had passed (Lev. 19:9–10), but Boaz tells his men, "Let her glean even *among* the sheaves, and do not reproach her. And also pull out some from the bundles for her, and leave it for her to glean, and do not rebuke her" (vv. 15–16). Later still, he sends Ruth home to Naomi with six full measures of barley, saying, according to Ruth, "You must not go back empty-handed to your mother-in-law" (3:17). Consistently he goes above and beyond what common courtesy or the law requires.

Which is not to say he doesn't manipulate. I find Boaz's handling of the next-of-kin in chapter 4 a masterpiece of strategy. He begins with an innocent invitation and a term of endearment ("Turn aside, friend; sit down here"), then summons the elders (vv. 1–2), thus disarming his "victim" while establishing the public forum needed to pressure him. He proceeds with a simple account of Naomi's plan to sell her land, adding almost off-handedly, "So I thought I would tell you of it, and say, Buy it in the presence of those sitting here, . . . for there is no one besides you to redeem it, and I come after you" (vv. 3–4). Only after the kinsman agrees to the purchase does Boaz mention that Ruth is part of the deal (v. 5). By separating the complication from the enticement he entraps his victim and ensures that he will back out, opening the way for Boaz to secure the land and marry Ruth—which is exactly what happens. The next-of-kin may have been ready to use others to his advantage, but Boaz fights fire with fire. He, too, manipulates, even using the kinsman as a "thing" (I-It), but for the ultimately good purpose of coming to Ruth's and Naomi's aid.

Which leads to Boaz's motives. I think these, like Naomi's, are mixed, but one predominates: Boaz relates to another because he responds to that other's goodness. When Ruth asks why she has found such favor in his eyes he tells her "All that you have done for your mother-in-law since the death of your husband has been fully told me, and how you left your father and mother and your native land and came to a people that you did not know before" (2:11). Later, on the threshing floor, when she asks him to spread his skirt over her (I will argue in a moment that Ruth is proposing to him here), he sees this as a sign of her honor and loyalty—"May you be blessed by the Lord, my daughter; you have made this last kindness greater than the first, in that you have not gone after young men, whether poor or rich" (3:10)—and quickly promises to work out the legal details that will enable them to marry. None of this denies, of course, that Boaz also has self-interest in mind. Ruth must be personally attractive to him: he tells her "all my fellow townsmen know that you are a woman of worth" (v. 11), and his first instructions, while suggesting concern for her safety and needs, also assure that he will not lose her to another landowner nor to the young men he has charged "not to molest" her (2:8–9). But by and large he relates by responding to her goodness.

Is his relationship consistent, or does it too undergo a change? I think it does develop, more subtly than Naomi's, but like hers in a positive direction. For Boaz's first response to Ruth is somewhat limited: he gives helpful instructions to her (2:8–9, 14) and to his workers (vv. 15–16), but does not put himself out; indeed, he "passes the buck" of personally aiding Ruth to his God: "*The Lord recompense you for what you have done, and a full reward be given you by the Lord*, the God of Israel, under whose wings you have come to take refuge" (2:12). But on the threshing floor, he goes further: still acknowledging the Lord ("May you be blessed by the Lord, my daughter"—3:10), he promises now to put himself on the line if needed, saying of the nearer kinsman: "if he will do the part of next of kin for you, well; let him do it; but if he is not willing . . . then, as the Lord lives, I will do the part of the next of kin for you" (v. 13). Next day he goes further still, insuring by his strategic moves that the next-of-kin will *not* "do the part" and paving the way for himself. He goes from indirect help to a qualified offer of personal help to an active seeking of her hand, progressing subtly but positively in his relationship to another.

What remains is to consider Ruth herself, for me one of the most intriguing characters in literature. On the surface she appears simple: totally selfless and innocent, passively trusting in the people and God of Israel. Yet underneath I find a subtle, complex, and fascinating human being.

She begins innocently enough, appearing to go above and beyond the call of duty in committing herself totally to Naomi, in contrast to the Orpah who has just returned to Moab. But has she really gone "above and beyond"? Is her attachment to Naomi selfless, or symbiotic? She is companion to her mother-in-law, true; but in return—unlike Orpah, who goes back alone in the world—she will have company, a roof over her head, a community to be part of, and a God whom she must know has provided food for his people (see 1:6). "For where you go I will go," she tells Naomi, "and where you lodge I will lodge; your people shall be my people, and your God my God" (1:16–17)—not just a selfless commitment (indeed, Naomi, wallowing in self-pity, may really want to be left alone as she has asked), but the determined pronouncement of a woman who knows what she needs as well as what she can give.

Ruth's complexity continues as we come to the question of manipulation. On the surface she appears victim, not perpetrator here—but look more closely. Chapter 2 begins with the narrator telling us, "Now Naomi had a kinsman of her husband's, a man of wealth, of the family of Elimelech, whose name was Boaz." In the very next verse Ruth says to Naomi, "Let me go to the field, and glean among the ears of grain *after him in whose sight I shall find favor.*" Is it just an accident, a stroke of fate, that she winds up in Boaz's field, or is the narrator being ironic when he says "she *happened* to come to" it (v. 3)? Is it possible Ruth knows about Boaz, that her act is a calculated attempt to bring about the desired result? Or, if she is not aware of this specific kinsman, is she nonetheless setting out to entice *somebody* to come to her aid? I don't think she is evil; in a man's world, this is how a woman must fend for herself. But neither do I find her passively innocent.

Her manipulation is clearer, I think, in the threshing floor scene.

Again Ruth seems passive; Naomi has given explicit instructions to which she has replied, "All that you say I will do" (3:5). And follow instructions she does—but not without adding something. Naomi had said "But when he lies down, observe the place where he lies; then go and uncover his feet and lie down; and *he will tell you what to do*" (v. 4). Ruth follows each step, except the last; instead of waiting for Boaz to give instructions, *she* tells him "spread your skirt over your maidservant, for you are next of kin" (v. 9). Such an act is tantamount to a proposal, or at least a demand for one (compare Ezek. 16:8). Naomi may be orchestrating the match, but Ruth does her part too, manipulating both Boaz and Naomi to produce the desired result.

What are Ruth's motives? Like those of others, I think they combine altruism and self-interest. In all she does—from insisting on remaining with Naomi to setting up the marriage with Boaz—she helps others, but also herself. And this leads to the final point: more than any other character, Ruth remains consistent in her relationships. She interplays selflessness and self-interest, passivity and action, subtlety and strength, throughout. She does not need to develop: from the beginning she allows the mask of innocence to hide her complex motives and behavior. What changes is my reader's perception of what she is doing, but I think she herself remains the same.

Reading the Book of Ruth makes me think in new and useful ways about how we relate to one another. I see different kinds of interpersonal relationships ranging from falling short of expectations to going above and beyond. I see everyone practicing a certain amount of manipulation, and it strikes me that this isn't always bad. I see different motives for relationships ranging from self-interest to concern for others, several characters combining both. I see people changing in interpersonal relationships, sometimes negatively, sometimes the opposite. For me this story again demonstrates how literary analysis of the Bible opens insights that illuminate and clarify experience.

XII
Ecclesiastes:
Disillusionment and Our
Philosophical Personality

(Ecclesiastes 1–12)

As human beings, we are each a complex of personalities. There is our psychological personality: we may be aggressive or laid back, spontaneous or rigid. There is our political personality: we may be conservative or liberal, reactionary or radical. There is our academic personality: we may be strong at math but weak with verbal skills, good at reading but poor in class discussion. Most of us, of course, are combinations of several traits in each category; indeed, we may vacillate from one trait to another at different times, though certain tendencies predominate.

I am convinced we all also possess another personality: a philosophical personality. We may be skeptics: doubting or questioning generally accepted conclusions. (I use *skeptic* and most of the following terms in broad, informal senses, not in reference to particular schools of philosophical thought.) We may be fatalists: resigning ourselves to a kind of predetermination, feeling caught up in an inescapable chain of events. We may be existentialists, emphasizing the isolation of our individual experiences in a hostile or indifferent universe; realists, inclined toward literal truth and pragmatism, toward an "honest" look at reality; agnostics, denying the possibility of real knowledge, especially regarding the existence of God.

Which label—or which combination of labels—applies to you? I think the answer is often revealed in the ways we react to moments of anguish and disillusionment. Consider a case in point: the parents of a baby victimized by sudden infant death syndrome, or crib death. Such parents may put a perfectly healthy child to bed at night and return next morning to find her lying lifeless in her crib, not a mark on her tiny body. Doctors are at a loss to explain the phenomenon. And being the parents of such a child must be a shattering, disillusioning experience. Think of such parents, say, six months after the death, when the initial shock has worn off. What are some ways you might expect them to react?

I can see some people growing very bitter, perhaps toward each other, perhaps toward the rest of the world. I can see others starting to question their earlier assumption that such catastrophes afflict only evil people. Still others may get angry at their doctor, or at God, for allowing this to happen. Some may be frustrated at their inability to understand what has happened; others may withdraw into a shell, feel cursed ("why has this happened to us?"), or shrug their shoulders in an "it's part of life" resignation. In another vein, some may plunge themselves into work or activity; some may seek a common bond with others, perhaps joining a community support group; some may even grow closer to their God. Indeed, individual parents will likely pass through a series of such reactions at different times.

Is it possible that such responses reveal underlying stances, suggest aspects of our philosophical personality? Questioning long-held assumptions, for example, may reflect, at least for the moment, a kind of skepticism. Feeling cursed may reveal at least a temporary touch of fatalism; shrugging one's shoulders, a dimension of realism. Anger at God, strangely enough, can suggest an underlying theism: a belief that God is real and is therefore somehow responsible for what has happened. Going into a shell, on the other hand, may indicate a kind of nihilism, a belief that nothing is of value any more.

The Book of Ecclesiastes strikes me as a series of journal-like reflections that reveal the philosophical personality of its primary narrator, the Preacher. (Another narrator seems to both introduce and conclude the book—see 1:1 and 12:9–14—but my concern is with the Preacher himself.) This Preacher is not responding to a single traumatic experience like a crib death; he has been disillusioned by life in general. Nonetheless, his comments suggest to me a series of definite philosophical stances. In studying them we may shed light on how as human beings we react to disillusionment and how we can detect our philosophical personalities.

What can we infer from the thoughts of this Preacher? For openers, I find his disillusionment leading to a strong note of skepticism, especially in the first two chapters. "Vanity of vanities, says the Preacher, vanity of vanities! All is vanity" (1:2). He then specifies exactly what he finds worthless, including in his list many things people have valued highly: wisdom (1:13–18), pleasure (2:1–3), striving for material possessions (2:4–8). Later he will sound particularly skeptical about what I have called retributive justice, arguing that, in contrast to much biblical teaching, there is no apparent connection between a person's behavior and reward: "In my vain life I have seen everything; there is a righteous man who perishes in his righteousness, and there is a wicked man who prolongs his life in his evil-doing" (7:15).

This last thought, in particular, leads the Preacher at times to a kind of fatalism, as he notes that success has little to do with skill, that the same impersonal forces govern all: "Again I saw that under the sun the race is not to the swift, nor the battle to the strong, nor bread to the wise, nor riches to the intelligent, nor favor to the men of skill; but time and chance happen to them all" (9:11). Earlier, this observation had led him to sense the futility of individual initiative in the face of fate: "What befalls the fool will befall me also; why then have I been so very wise?" (2:15). Indeed, near the beginning of his reflections, he had hinted at the nature of this impersonal fate: it is a cyclical force, making all things move in ever-repeating circles, with no clear opportunity for escape:

> The sun rises and the sun goes down,
>   and hastens to the place where it rises.
> The wind blows to the south,
>   and goes round to the north;
> round and round goes the wind,
>   and on its circuits the wind returns.
> All streams run to the sea,
>   but the sea is not full;
> to the place where the streams flow,
>   there they flow again. (1:5–7)

At still other moments I think the Preacher espouses a kind of existentialism, sensing the isolation of his experience in a world whose cosmic nature is uncertain, if not devoid of meaning. This causes him to focus only on his earthly existence (an attitude stressed through the repeated phrase "under the sun"), since anything else is at best beyond his grasp: "Who knows whether the spirit of man goes upward and the spirit of the beast goes down to the earth? So I saw that there is nothing better than that a man should enjoy his work, for that is his lot; who can bring him to see what will be after him?" (3:21–22). Later thoughts of Sheol, the Hebrew abode of the dead, simply confirm his worst suspicions and reinforce his emphasis on present existence. This is hinted at in verses like 9:5–6, but made most explicit in 9:10: "Whatever your hand finds to do, do it with your might; for there is no work or thought or knowledge or wisdom in Sheol, to which you are going." Many readers are surprised at the contrast between later concepts of the afterlife and that which pervades this book, but the Preacher, lacking a sure, meaningful afterlife, thinks not of his position in the cosmos. He tries to make the most of his present existence before it's too late.

Such concentration on existence may lead naturally to another facet of the Preacher's philosophical personality: he often seems to me a realist, attempting an honest look at life and drawing practical conclusions from it. He puts aside rose-colored glasses, looking squarely at the pain and suffering that permeate life, and responding sensitively to them (for example, 4:1ff.). Yet he also acknowledges that such negatives can be countered by better things, a balanced worldview nowhere better expressed than in the famous poem that opens chapter 3. Here the Preacher observes that good and evil, joy and sorrow, pleasure and pain, come in pairs; so there is a time to be born as well as to die, a time to plant as well as "to pluck up what is planted," a time to heal as well as to kill. This realism produces a practical view of life, a pragmatism best seen in the many proverbs and maxims that give the flavor of down-home wisdom to the book. Some reinforce attitudes we've already seen ("there is nothing new under the sun"—1:9), but most offer practical advice drawn from the Preacher's hard look at the world:

"There is nothing better for a man than that he should eat and drink, and find enjoyment in his toil" (2:24); "Be not rash with your mouth, nor let your heart be hasty to utter a word before God, for God is in heaven, and you upon earth; therefore let your words be few" (5:2); "It is better for a man to hear the rebuke of the wise than to hear the song of fools" (7:5). Such observations suggest to me a human being who has drawn realistically from his experience.

And yet that experience has not satisfied the Preacher, for it has failed to answer his deepest questions. So I find him venturing often into a special brand of agnosticism—not struggling with the existence of God, but with his inability to understand life, to grasp what that God is and has produced. Notice how much frustration he feels at the limits on human knowledge: "For who knows what is good for man while he lives the few days of his vain life, which he passes like a shadow? For who can tell man what will be after him under the sun?" (6:12); "All this I have tested by wisdom; I said, 'I will be wise'; but it was far from me. That which is, is far off, and deep, very deep; who can find it out?" (7:23–24); "Then I saw all the work of God, that man cannot find out the work that is done under the sun. However much man may toil in seeking, he will not find it out; even though a wise man claims to know, he cannot find it out" (8:17). This agnosticism feeds back into attitudes I noted earlier, such as his skeptical attitude toward wisdom and his existential sense of isolation in the universe. So I find the Preacher, like most human beings, vacillating from one position to another, moving back and forth among stances not totally separate. Like a diamond rotating in the light, he reveals first one facet, then another, then yet another, though all are part of the same stone.

Thus the Preacher's philosophical personality seems to me characterized, at one time or another, by skepticism, fatalism, existentialism, realism, and agnosticism. But these all sound bleak; is he optimistic about anything? I think we have already seen that the answer must be yes. For one thing, the Preacher often qualifies his thoughts: though he may criticize a concept at one moment, at another he will reveal that he does not find it totally worthless:

compare his comment on wisdom at 1:18 with that at 7:19. Again, he acknowledges a time for pleasant things in life: to build up, to laugh, to dance, to gather stones together, to embrace, to seek, to keep, to sew, to speak, to love, to enjoy peace (3:1–8). He admits that things could sometimes be worse: "Two are better than one, because they have a good reward for their toil. For if they fall, one will lift up his fellow; but woe to him who is alone when he falls and has not another to lift him up" (4:9–10). He commends enjoyment, espousing an almost epicurean "eat, drink, and be merry" attitude (for example, 8:15). And he remains always a theist, never—even in his deepest gloom—doubting the existence of a God, indeed sometimes finding a kind of consolation in him: "I know that whatever God does endures for ever; nothing can be added to it, nor anything taken from it; God has made it so, in order that men should fear before him" (3:14).

The Preacher does, in short, accentuate the positive, perhaps more often than we give him credit for. And yet, it seems to me, his optimism is always tempered; he embraces nothing as an absolute good. Thus wisdom may give strength to the wise (7:19), but remember that it produces much vexation (1:18). There is a time for pleasant things in life, but each is balanced by a negative (3:1–8). There is good in two people coming together, but only *relative* good: "Two are better than one" (4:9). There is value in enjoyment, but only by default: people should eat, drink, and enjoy themselves because there is nothing better (8:15). And there is a God in his heaven, but that's the problem: he's up there, and we're down here, and what he is really like we do not know: "But all this I laid to heart, examining it all, how the righteous and the wise and their deeds are in the hand of God; whether it is love or hate man does not know" (9:1). The Preacher is not a nihilist, embracing nothing; indeed, no single label will suffice for him. But his stances are permeated by pessimism, and what good he sees is always quickly qualified.

I've often wondered how the Preacher would react to a single traumatic experience like a crib death. Very likely he would run through a series of responses, as most of us do; in fact, the slipperiness of the terms I've tried to describe him with, the tendency of one label to blend into the next, reminds me of the dangers of categorizing and oversimplifying. But again, he has been burned, not by one incident, but by life in general. He has left us a record, a kind of journal, of his responses. Running throughout is a strong note of disillusionment: this Preacher will no longer easily accept pious platitudes about the world. But like the light on the rotating diamond, that disillusionment reveals facets of his philosophical personality. Though my analysis, as always, is meant to be suggestive, not exhaustive, I hope we've seen enough to get a feel for the sensitivity and complexity of the human being who stands behind this work.

One final note. People sometimes ask if a work of prose discourse like Ecclesiastes is really literature. We may have arrived at an answer. If in reading the text of this book we find a pattern of philosophical stances taken by a person reacting to disillusionment, and if that pattern helps sharpen our insights about similar experiences—whether specific traumas like crib death or general confrontations with life—then Ecclesiastes fits my definition quite well. More important, it puts us in touch with a sensitive person from long ago who, like us, was trying to get a better grasp on the human predicament.

The New Testament

XIII

The Good Samaritan: A Question of Ethics

(Luke 10:25 –37)

You are driving along a deserted highway late one evening when you spot a stranded motorist by the side of the road. The man appears injured, his car damaged. No one else is in sight. Do you stop to help, or drive on? If you stop, you put yourself in danger: another car might strike you by accident. Or you could spring a trap: six hoodlums might be hiding behind the bushes waiting to jump you. Besides, another vehicle may come by in a few moments—a police car or ambulance, someone better equipped to help. And yet. . . .

The moral question of how a human being is supposed to behave toward others is one of the most profound and enduring of issues. The Greeks developed an entire branch of philosophy—ethics—around it. Much of the Torah—indeed, of the entire Hebrew Bible—expounds upon it. It is an issue frequently addressed by Jesus, in the Sermon on the Mount, in various discourses—and in the parable of the Good Samaritan.

There is an argument among biblical scholars about how best to read a parable. Some say it should be read as allegory, with each detail—right down to the "two denarii" the Samaritan gives as payment to the innkeeper—standing for something in the outside world. Others argue for the method of analogy, with the parable establishing an implicit comparison between its own story and one central point Jesus wants to communicate: that point here might be how best to love your neighbor. I think there is truth in both camps and that the "best" method depends on several factors, including the length of the parable (longer ones often seem more amenable to allegorical interpretation; shorter ones, to analogy). But for many parables, I prefer a method that mediates between the extremes—the same method I have used throughout this study

91

to read other biblical material. This means we must begin with the parable's text, infer from it one or more patterns, then use those patterns to help clarify our own understanding of experience.

To apply all this to the parable of the Good Samaritan, let's begin by reading carefully Luke 10:25—37. Note that I am including the conversations that precede and follow the parable proper and thus establish its context. That context, we are told, involves a lawyer (not a civil professional, but one who might study the law of Moses) who has asked what he must do to inherit eternal life. In response to Jesus' questions, he reveals that he knows the two great commandments: to love God with everything you have, "and your neighbor as yourself" (v. 27). Jesus tells him he is correct. But the lawyer wants to "justify himself." Observe carefully the form of his second question: "And who is my neighbor?" (v. 29)—that is, toward what kind of person ought I direct the love called for in the great commandment? In response, Jesus begins his story.

Some background information will help us better understand the parable's text. The narrative begins on the road between Jerusalem and Jericho, a place notorious for its "highway robbers" (observe how this detail helps make the plot realistic, a characteristic of most parables). The priest and the Levite who pass by the robbers' victim are important members of the religious hierarchy who undoubtedly know if they touch a corpse they will be unclean and unfit for Temple service—and we have been told that the man was left "half dead" (v. 30). The Samaritan (the text never calls him "good") is a hated foreigner, a descendant of those northern Israelites who intermarried with Gentiles after the Assyrian conquest in the eighth century B.C.E. A severe split between Samaritans and Jews occurred several centuries before Jesus' time, and each group suspected and detested the other. All this notwithstanding, note how this Samaritan ministers to the wounded man, carries him on his own beast, looks after him at the inn, pays the innkeeper, and offers to pay more if necessary—all for a complete stranger.

Also pay close attention to the question Jesus poses to the lawyer at the conclusion of the parable: "Which of these three, do you think, proved neighbor to the man who fell among the robbers?" (v. 36). The lawyer apparently finds it a simple question, for he replies without hesitation: "The one who showed mercy on him," to which Jesus answers, "Go and do likewise." I'll return to all this in a moment.

Now let's turn to one of the parable's implicit patterns: the question of ethical behavior. Perhaps we can begin with the lawyer's question: "And who is my neighbor?" How has Jesus answered it? I used to think, by implying that "he who is in need is my neighbor," or by extension, "each person, regardless of nationality, is my neighbor." But I've come to see this parable in a new and exciting light, and I now wonder if such answers aren't missing the central thrust.

To be sure, I find several things going on here. Some suggest *in*appropriate forms of behavior, ethical "traps" we fall into. For example, the parable says to me that those who are nominally "people of God"—the first two who pass by the wounded man— don't always behave in the best way, that taking solace in belonging to the right group is not enough. It also suggests that those who are members of the religious hierarchy—the priest and the Levite— don't always behave in the best way. (Note that the Samaritan seems to hold no ecclesiastical office; he is presented as a lay person.) It even implies that those who are following what they consider a valid religious practice—avoiding contact with the dead to remain ritually pure—don't always behave in the best way, that indeed, following a religious rule may interfere with obedience to the higher rule of love.

On the more positive side, I think the story says better behavior may sometimes be found among religious "outsiders" like the Samaritan. It implies that love transcends religious and national boundaries: the Samaritan does not ask the victim's ancestry or affiliation before helping. And it suggests such love may well involve what we would normally consider imprudent and preposterous behavior. For the Samaritan does not stop to wonder whether he is in danger, whether the man lying by the road is the bait for a trap. He does not simply walk over and offer assistance. He does everything, and then some—from touching the wounds and bathing them with oil and wine, to making an open-ended offer to pay all the bills. His behavior is, to be sure, almost insane.

But we have not yet come to what I think is the parable's central point. The lawyer had begun by acknowledging that the road to eternal life is partly followed by loving one's neighbor as oneself. He had then asked, "Who is my neighbor?"—who should be the *object* of my love? His question may well imply that he expects a limiting answer: you must love these groups of people here, but you can forget those over there and over there. And I used to think the parable destroyed this presumption by answering "anyone in need is your neighbor." But this misses the point, for in fact the parable does *not* answer the lawyer's question at all! It implies that his question—about the proper objects of love—is in fact the wrong question. It turns that question on its head by answering a different, better one—the one posed by Jesus when his story is done: "Which of these three, do you think, *proved neighbor to* the man who fell among the robbers?" This is not a restatement of the lawyer's query, for it is about the *subject,* not the objects, of love. The appropriate question, Jesus seems to say, is not "*Whom* should I love?" but "How can *I* go about loving?" It is a question about the self. And once we recognize it, the answer seems clear, even to the lawyer: people can go about loving by imitating the Samaritan, by transcending boundaries, by giving of themselves in an imprudent, preposterous, insane way.

I think the parable of the Good Samaritan is a beautiful story, but not for the usually understood reasons. It is beautiful, not because every detail stands for something else, not because it makes only one major point, but because it turns the lawyer's world—and our own—upside down. We have trouble behaving properly toward others, it seems to say, because we put our trust in the right group, the right hierarchy, the prescribed practices. We could do better to imitate behavior often found outside the mainstream, to ignore traditional boundaries, traditional notions of what is prudent and safe. But most of all, we would do better to no longer ask the wrong question, to switch our attention from the objects to the subjects of love.

When we come to relate this pattern to our experience, we may discover recognizable phenomena. How many people do we know who consider themselves superior to others because they belong to the "right church"? How many who adhere scrupulously to religious ritual and ignore the cry in the street? How many—including ourselves—who seek to impose limits on love, excluding certain people and avoiding foolishly excessive self-giving? A literary reading of the parable of the Good Samaritan allows us to think about such issues in different, profoundly significant ways.

XIV

The Prodigal Son: Family Jealousies and Justice

(Luke 15:11–32)

I have a brother, six years younger than myself, with whom I now get along pretty well. But in our childhood years, we had our share of squabbles. I remember being bothered, for example, by the issue of bedtimes: he was allowed to stay up later, it seemed to me, than I had been at the same age. He had fewer household chores, I thought, and he always got the presents he asked for; I recall believing this so much that once, when I wanted a puppy, I tried to talk *him* into asking for it, sensing a greater chance of success. (The ploy didn't work.)

From today's perspective,, all this seems embarrassingly trivial. Yet it represents a typical case of a universal phenomenon: sibling jealousy. Most of us have felt victimized in comparison to brothers and sisters. Usually we perceive this as a case of injustice: we have been treated unfairly, we believe, either by siblings themselves, or by parents. The theme pervades much literature; it runs like a thread, in fact through Genesis, in the stories of Cain and Abel, Jacob and Esau, Leah and Rachel, Joseph and his brothers. It appears, too, in the New Testament, perhaps nowhere more prominently than in the parable of the Prodigal Son, a story that wrestles with the questions of how family members—not only siblings, but parents and children—relate to one another, and what kinds of injustice they sometimes encounter.

As we approach this parable, I think we should once again take note of its context. In Luke 15 Jesus is accused of associating with riffraff (vv. 1–2). He responds with three parables about things that are lost: a lost sheep (vv. 3–7), a lost coin (8–10), and finally, a lost son (11–32; perhaps, from the son's perspective, "a lost home"). Each seems designed, on one level, to answer Jesus' accusers' implied belief that it is inappropriate, even unjust, to "receive sinners and eat with them."

The text of the Prodigal Son is, like that of other parables, often realistic, if not mundane. Jewish fathers, for example, typically divided their property between sons; the younger's share, in this case, would be about one-third. Palestinian Jews also frequently emigrated to Gentile countries, as the younger son seems to do. The parable has clear points of drama as well, however. The lost son's degradation is pointedly shown when he is forced to tend swine (v. 15), an act abhorrent to a Jew. And the father's response to this son's return—he calls for "the best robe," a ring, shoes, and the fatted calf for a feast (vv. 22–23)—goes beyond expectations: clearly, the son is not only restored, but honored, making his brother's reaction (vv. 25–30) understandable.

Now let's examine the pattern of intrafamily relationships. First the narrative focuses on the father and his younger son. This father begins, it would seem, with simple justice: upon request he gives his son, without hesitation or quibbling, his share of the property—nothing more, nothing less (v. 12). But he also grants a less tangible gift: freedom. The son is not hindered in his decision to leave, is not discouraged even from turning that liberty into license as he goes through his property "in loose living" (v. 13). But the father is not yet finished; he will add a still more subtle gift: patience. For he simply waits while the son encounters the real world experience of an empty pocket and a great famine, while the boy has to work for a living at the most degrading of jobs, in the depths of hunger and want (vv. 14–16). He waits, in fact, for his child to make the first move.

In a few simple verses, then, the father provides more than property; he demonstrates justice, freedom, and patience for his offspring. Now it is the son's turn to respond, and he does so on two levels. First he evidences an internal change: he "comes to himself" and realizes he cannot continue apart from his family, that there is a place for him, however humble, at home. "How many of my father's hired servants have bread enough and to spare, but I perish here with hunger!" he says (v. 17). He decides not to seek reinstatement, for that would be unjust, so he assumes a humble pose and rehearses a little speech: "Father, I have sinned against heaven and before you; I am no longer worthy to be called your son; treat me as one of your hired servants" (v. 19). Thus prepared, he demonstrates his external change, arising and reversing his earlier journey by returning home (v. 20a).

But the father will not wait for all this to happen: at the first sign of his son's return, he offers yet another gift: immediate compassion. While the son is "yet at a distance," we are told—and before he has a chance to utter a word—"his father saw him and had compassion, and ran and embraced him and kissed him" (v. 20b). Indeed, the son begins his prepared speech, but before he can finish, his father, apparently not even listening, provides the boy with his final gift: honor. It is a gift almost insanely excessive, for this father (like the Good Samaritan) offers more than could be reasonably expected. The son, avoiding a plea for injustice, asked for less than full restoration, but the father—with his best robe and ring and shoes and fatted calf—provides more. Indeed, he gives more than the material items on this list, for to them we must add the justice, freedom, patience, compassion, and honor the parable has implied. The father, in fact, inverts the mandate to "Honor your father and your mother"—one of the Ten Commandments that form the cornerstone of biblical justice. Paradoxically, he both practices and subverts that justice. Yet his gifts, coupled with the son's internal and external changes, are fit cause for the merriment now celebrated. Like the man with his sheep and the woman with her coin, this father now knows the joy of finding what seemed lost: "Let us eat and make merry," he says, "for this my son was dead, and is alive again; he was lost, and is found" (vv. 23–24).

But the parable is not yet over. For the narrative now turns to the father and his elder son, a relationship brought to a crisis by the return of the younger. (Interestingly, the brothers never come near one another in this story; it is their father through whom their relationship is expressed.) We find the elder son "in the field" (v. 25)—in the place of work, while his brother has been at play. He returns to the sounds of music and dancing, an atmosphere unfamiliar to him since he must ask a servant for an explanation (v. 26). When he receives it, his feelings come to the surface: "he was angry and refused to go in" (v. 28a).

Then the father does something noteworthy: he goes out and entreats the boy (v. 28b). Again he reverses the expected parent-child relationship, the one implied in the "just" Commandment. He responds, in fact, more quickly to this son than he had to the other; he does not even wait for the boy to make a first move.

But the elder, in his anger, can see none of this. In his view, he has been treated unfairly, unjustly, in relation to his brother, and he says so straight out: "Lo, these many years I have served you, and I never disobeyed your command: yet you never gave me a kid, that I might make merry with my friends. But when this son of yours came [he cannot even call the boy his brother], who has devoured your living with harlots, you killed for him the fatted calf!" (vv. 29–30). Never have I seen a clearer example of sibling jealousy, a more straightforward statement of a brother's belief that he is a victim of injustice.

Which leads to a central question. Is the elder brother right? Has the father been fair and just? This has to be given, I think, two answers. On the one hand, the father has been extremely just. He began by dividing his property between his sons according to their customary shares, giving not only to the younger who asked for it, but also to the elder (v. 12b: "And he divided his living between them"). He has given material gifts to the younger son—again, the robe, ring, shoes, and fatted calf—but also to the elder; as he now says, "Son, you are always with me, and all that is mine is yours" (v. 31). He has given intangible gifts to the younger—but also to the elder, whom he treats with gentleness and compassion and great patience, whom he goes out and entreats without even waiting for a first move, as he had with his younger. He has, in short, been quite fair, demonstrating a justice to which the elder son has been blinded by anger.

Yet in another sense, I have to agree with the elder son: his father has not been just. Justice in its simplest sense—what I have called retributive justice—means rewards for good behavior, punishment for bad. The younger son has behaved foolishly, at the very least, and does not deserve the reception he gets, a notion he himself recognizes in asking only to be treated as a hired servant. The elder son has apparently worked diligently and deserves a greater reward. But the father recognizes a notion neither of his sons may yet know: there is something more important than being fair. He is less concerned with justice than with redemption, with reestablishing broken ties, with reclaiming that which was lost. And so the parable ends with his proclaiming; "It was fitting to make merry and be glad, for this your brother [not 'my son,' notice, but 'your brother'] was dead, and is alive; he was lost, and is found" (v. 32).

The parable of the Good Samaritan turns the world on its head by transforming the lawyer's question—"Who is my neighbor?"—into a better one: "How can I be neighbor to another?" The parable of the Prodigal Son, I think, does the same by transforming the implied notion of the Pharisees and scribes—"It is unjust to receive and eat with sinners" (see v. 2)—into two more important notions: justice may be present where the blind don't perceive it, and better yet, justice is less important than reclamation. Justice means if you lose your sheep, your coin, your son, or your home, that's tough—you've got to face the consequences. Reclamation means you go beyond justice to a greater joy than the simply just can ever know.

The parable reminds me, in short, that the perceived injustice leading to sibling jealousy is both imaginary and real: parents often treat their children more fairly than the children recognize, but more important, parents may know that treating them fairly isn't always the highest good. For some, these implications go well beyond a human family: if God is a parent, then his treatment of his children may be clarified, for them, by this reading. But on whatever level, the parable gives us cause to stop and ponder experience in a new light—the ultimate value, I believe, of reading good literature.

XV

Acts of the Apostles:
The Archetypal Birthing Process

(Acts 1–15)

Here are two questions about two different kinds of "parents":

1. What do all natural mothers share in common? Answer: the birth of a baby. Without getting overly technical, it is obvious that new life is conceived in their wombs and that some form of growth and development (gestation) takes place within them, usually culminating in labor and delivery.
2. What do the following "fathers" share in common: Martin Luther, John Calvin, Henry VIII, John Wesley, Joseph Smith? Answer: the birth of a "new" religion. To be sure, each would argue that he did not start a *new* religion but purified and preserved the old (more on that later). But in the popular mind, at least, they are seen as the founding fathers of five forms of Christianity: the Lutheran, Presbyterian, Anglican, Methodist, and Mormon churches.

I think both questions deal with what some have called an *archetype*—a repeated pattern of human experience often illustrated in myth, ritual, and literature. I call this particular archetype the birthing process. It is archetypal in two senses. Physically, we all go through it; indeed, the only way to get into the world is to pass through some sort of conception-gestation-delivery. But we also witness it socially, in many situations: branch campuses are "spawned" by major universities, new nations emerge from "mother" countries, new denominations are "born" from established religions. These "social births," it seems to me, often follow a process analogous to their physical counterparts.

Among other things, the first half of Acts depicts another instance of this archetype: the emergence of Christianity from

101

"mother" Judaism. I think this, too, is a birthing process, complete with a moment of conception, several stages of gestation, and delivery. Of course it is not a physical process, but a social one, most closely resembling other social births.

I would like to consider nine facets of this process, arranged into categories as follows:

Category	Facet	
I. Conception	1. Moment of Conception	
II. Gestation	2. Initial Peace and Harmony	
	3. Rapid Growth	9. Greater Power in Control
	4. Specialization	
	5. Modeling the Founder	
	6. Problems from Without	
	7. Problems from Within	
III. Delivery	8. Separation from Source	

(I want to call them facets rather than stages or steps, for while they are distinctly recognizable parts of the whole, they do not necessarily occur in discrete sequential units.) For each I'll attempt four things: to label the facet, briefly cite a physical analogue (using human birth as an example), briefly cite a social analogue (using the emergence of later denominations from "mother" Christianity as an example), and finally, demonstrate the facet's presence in the Book of Acts. When we're done, we may have sharpened our awareness, not only of the historical origins of Christianity, but of the birthing process itself, both its physical and social forms.

Facet one involves a moment of conception. Physical birthing processes clearly begin with such a moment; social births often start when an idea is conceived in one or more minds (so Lutheranism may be said to have begun when Martin Luther was inspired by passages in Paul's letters; Mormonism, when Joseph Smith experienced a vision in the early ninetenth century). In Acts, I think conception occurs at Pentecost as the Holy Spirit descends on a small group of Jesus' disciples who are gathered together (2:1–4). The event recalls an earlier, physical conception when the same

Spirit descends on Mary (Luke 1:35). Such moments involve mystical unions between natural and supernatural, paradoxically reminding me of the medically explainable yet ultimately ineffable nature of physical conception, of the mysterious convergence of rational mind and nonrational inspiration during its social analogue.

In facet two of the birthing process, the long period of gestation begins as initial peace and harmony prevail both within and without the new phenomenon. In the weeks following conception, the tiny embryo is a relatively simple organism developing so slowly and quietly that it is hardly noticed—indeed, may be totally unnoticed—by its mother. Similarly, the first Mormons were a small cohesive group virtually unnoticed by mainline Christianity. In Acts, we learn that the first Christians number only about 120 people (1:15) and that even as they grow they remain simple and get along beautifully: "And they devoted themselves to the apostles' teaching and fellowship, to the breaking of bread and the prayers. . . . And all who believed were together and had all things in common; and they sold their possessions and goods and distributed them to all, as any had need" (2:42–45; cf. 4:32–37). We are also told that they continue to observe Jewish practices, worshiping daily in the Temple, and that they have "favor with all the people" (2:46–47). In short, there are no significant problems from within or without the group.

In facet three, the phenomenon experiences rapid growth, as the embryo grows rapidly into a fetus, as a new denomination attracts more and more members. In Acts, part of this growth is reflected in numbers: 3,000 are added to the group after Peter's first sermon (2:41), and after Peter and John's arrest, the number of men has grown to around 5,000 (4:4). But expansion is also suggested in geographical area: the movement that had begun in Jerusalem soon spreads into other districts of Judea and into Samaria (8:1ff.), and then into Gentile territory (11:19–21). Paul's journeys will carry the word throughout most of the known world, including Rome; thus what had started in the hinterlands (the Mormon church originated in a small town in upstate New York) expands to wider and wider regions.

In facet four, the principle of specialization sets in as a power structure is solidified and a hierarchy established. In the developing fetus, the brain begins to coordinate as body parts and organs become distinguishable and begin their separate functions; in a new denomination, a leadership is established and specific tasks assigned. In Acts, despite the harmony of the community, authority clearly rests in a small, separate, self-preserving group of twelve; I find it interesting that upon Judas's death, his position there must immediately be filled (1:15–26), the distinction between leaders and masses preserved. Later, the apostles will institute a division of labor, appointing a group of seven to deal with the distribution of goods while they devote themselves "to prayer and to the ministry of the word" (6:2–4). Later still, Paul and Barnabas will set up hierarchies in the communities they establish (for example, see 14:23). The earlier emphasis on equality and the sharing of a common lot (review 4:32–37) gives way, subtly yet perceptibly, to an all-too-familiar power strucure.

As we approach facet five, we find the new phenomenon more and more clearly modeling its founder. A developing fetus takes on genetic and physical characteristics of its parents; members of a new social movement often imitate their founder (virtually all new Christian denominations claim to be following Jesus more precisely than their predecessors). In Acts, I'm impressed by how much individual Christians begin to speak, act, and get treated like Jesus. In the Gospels, Peter is anything but an eloquent speaker; during Jesus' transfiguration, for example, he blurts out an apparently silly comment, "not knowing what he said" (Luke 9:33). But now, the old fisherman delivers lengthy and powerful sermons, interpreting the Hebrew Bible with a vigor and insight rivaling the scribes and Pharisees—just like Jesus. The follower and his founder become less and less distinguishable.

But this modeling phenomenon is not limited to leaders among the twelve. The martyr Stephen, for example, is arrested and accused in much the same manner—and for much the same reasons—as Jesus had been: he performs signs and wonders that disturb some people, who stir up the masses and their leaders so that Stephen is dragged before the Council, where he is attacked by false witnesses and accused of blasphemy (6:8–14). Interestingly, among Stephen's final words as he is executed are "Lord Jesus, receive my spirit" and "Lord, do not hold this sin against them" (7:59, 60), both clearly evoking Jesus' words on the cross (Luke 23:34, 46). As part of its gestation process, the Christian community assumes more and more characteristics of its founder.

In facet six, the new phenomenon must deal increasingly with problems from without. A fetus must interact with the environment provided by its mother; its movements occasionally cause her discomfort, and her behavior (diet, motion, emotional state) inevitably affect it. Socially, a new movement will eventually come into conflict with the outside world; so medieval Lutherans accused Catholics of wrongly defining and interpreting the Bible, while Catholics accused these new Protestants of the same. In Acts, I find a hint of this facet immediately following the Pentecost experience, as Jews begin to think the disciples strange and ill-mannered. How can these people speak simultaneously in different languages, they wonder; indeed, some suspect they are drunk (2:5–13). Soon, arguments develop from both directions. Peter repeatedly accuses his own people of responsibility for Jesus' death (see 3:13); conversely, Jewish leaders arrest Peter and John for proclaiming the Resurrection (4:1–3). The peace and harmony of earlier days in soon shattered, the antagonism culminating in violence (8:1).

Which brings us to facet seven: the new phenomenon confronts problems from within. A baby must interact not only with its mother but with itself, struggling to achieve proper hormonal balance and the right interdependence of bodily functions. Members of new social movements don't always agree; early followers of Luther and Calvin, for example, argued over several issues before branching off in separate directions, and squabbles among Anglicans led to three editions of their Book of Common Prayer within ten years. In Acts, I find such internal dissension arising from a variety of causes. There is disagreement stemming partly from nationality: so Hellenists murmur against Hebrews in 6:1. There is conflict over material goods; the Hellenist-Hebrew argument is over daily distribution to widows. There is envy of power: the recently converted Simon offers to buy the apostles' power to convey the Spirit by laying on of hands, inciting Peter to indignant anger (8:18–24). There is dissension caused by suspicion: former enemy Saul is not well received by Jerusalem Christians (9:26). There is disagreement over an issue: church leaders assemble in full council to decide whether Gentile converts must submit to Jewish circumcision before becoming Christians—that is, whether Christianity is yet a sect of Judaism, or a distinct religion (chapter 15). Finally, there is dissension that appears to stem from personality and pride; so Paul and Barnabas split over the question of John Mark's accompanying them on their second journey (15:36–41). Like peaceful relations with outsiders, the internal harmony of earlier days proves a temporary stage; human nature being what it is, strife among the members seems inevitable.

Birthing processes may seem never-ending, but they eventually reach a climax. In this scheme, the climax comes in facet eight, as the new phenomenon finally separates from its source. For a baby this means delivery, the birth itself. For a social movement, it means the irrevocable break with the past, the cutting, if you will, of the umbilical cord (perhaps Martin Luther's formal excommunication from the Catholic church, with its full consequences not only for himself but also for his followers). In Acts, as in these parallel examples, however, this facet seems to me not so much a single dramatic moment as the end result of a continual movement toward separation.

Christianity had clearly begun as part of Judaism. The first Christians remained devout Jews who attempted to radicalize—literally, get back to the root of—the Jewish tradition in light of the Christian message. Peter explained the Pentecost experience as a fulfillment of the Hebrew Bible (2:15ff.). Stephen began his speech with a long summary of Jewish biblical tradition (7:1ff.). Peter, John, and others worshiped regularly in the Temple (for example, 3:1). Even Paul and his companions, on their missionary journeys, took seats in the local synagogues on the Sabbath, and when they spoke, based their message on Jewish Scripture (see 13:13ff.). In this they resembled Wesley's early attempts, not to break from the Anglican Church, but to reform it from within.

More and more, however, the language of these Christians suggests their growing awareness that a break from mother Judaism must come. In the synagogue at Antioch of Pisidia, for instance, Paul begins by exhorting the assembled Jews, but ends in quite a different vein. "It was necessary that the word of God should be spoken first to you," he says, but then adds "Since you thrust it from you, and judge yourselves unworthy of eternal life, behold, we turn to the Gentiles" (13:46). This notion that Christianity will leave Judaism behind grows throughout Acts, as the Christian movement, which had begun strongly tied to the establishment religion, breaks with more and more traditional practices (like circumcision), and devotes more and more attention to Gentiles.

Paradoxically, however, Acts continually stresses that even while separating from its source, Christianity has not diverged from Judaism but become its rightful heir, other Jews having forsaken their heritage (see Paul's final speech to the Jewish leaders of Rome, 28:25–28). Similarly, one might argue that a baby is not so much a "new" phenomenon as a fulfillment of, and heir to, its parents, a new denomination not really a break with the past but a fulfillment of tradition apostatized by others (as almost every reformer has claimed). Still, the sense of separation between what is new and what immediately came before seems real to me. A newborn baby, a new denomination, and early Christianity are each delivered from a womb, separated from its mother, recognized as a distinct entity.

There remains one last facet in my scheme, different from the others in that it seems less a stage (though no facet has been a clearly definable stage) and more a pervasive presence, a quality infusing the whole process. It is the overriding sense that a greater power has been in control throughout. Few who experience the conception, gestation, and delivery of a baby fail to sense the far-from-totally explainable "miracle" of it all. Few who participate in any denomination fail to believe the emergence of their sect was far from an accident, was somehow meant to be. And so in Acts I find this pervasive presence in, for example, the miracles that help the new movement along. There are miracles involving human intermediaries, as we have seen (so Peter raised Tabitha from the dead), but more to the point are those that just "happen." The Holy Spirit miraculously descends at Pentecost to start the ball rolling (2:1–4). Saul is dramatically blinded on the road to Damascus (9:1–9), and God explains that this former enemy "is a chosen instrument of mine to carry my name before the Gentiles and kings and the sons of Israel" (v. 15). Imprisoned apostles are freed by "an angel of the Lord" (5:17–21). Another angel frees Peter from Herod Agrippa (12:1ff.), then smites the king "because he did not give God the glory" (12:23). This sense of supernatural control will continue throughout Acts (note the role of the Holy Spirit, and of a vision, in directing missionaries in 16:6–10). It places the emergence of Christianity squarely in the hands of a supernatural providence.

The birth of the Christian movement in Acts, then, seems to me a process with nine recognizable dimensions, all but the last grouped under one of three headings: (1) a moment of conception; (2) a long gestation period that begins in peace and harmony, then moves through rapid growth, development of specialized functions, a tendency to model the founder, a need to deal with problems from without and from within; and (3) a delivery through which it is separated from its "mother"—all in the hands of a pervasive greater power. I find it an archetypal experience, paralleling physical birth and the emergence of social institutions: not only later Christian denominations, of course, but many new groups emerging from ones that preceded them. Viewed as history, Acts gives us primary information about the origin of a major world religion; viewed as literature, it adds to that an intriguing perspective on births of many kinds.

XVI

Revelation:
"The Sense of an Ending"

(Revelation 1–22)

Probably no biblical book has inspired more ambivalent reader reaction than Revelation. Here is a work that intrigues as it mystifies,
entices as it frightens. Naturally, there has been a host of interpretations over the centuries, most, I think, falling into one of two
camps.

One camp reads the work historically—typically, as an attempt
to encourage early Christian perseverance under cruel treatment by
first-century Roman Emperors. Proponents cite its continual promise of the replacement of an era of oppression and violence by a
new order of righteousness and peace (a typical concern of apocalyptic literature, of which Revelation is a prime example), as well
as its emphasis on the value of martyrdom (for instance, 20:4–6).
The other camp reads the work futuristically, usually as a prediction of the end of the world scheduled for the reader's own lifetime.
Virtually every generation for the past two thousand years has produced futuristic readers; in the twentieth century alone, the "beast"
of Revelation 13 (which historicists claim represents Rome) has
been identified as Adolf Hitler, Nikita Khrushchev, even Nelson
Rockefeller.

It seems to me, however, that extremists in both camps suffer
from the same important limitation: they assume the "real meaning" of Revelation, its ultimate referent, is a single, one-time event.
For historicists, this event (perhaps first-century Roman persecu-
tion) took place long ago during the time of the book's writer; the
message for today is confined to historical curiosity. For futurists,
the ultimate referent will occur for the first and only time during
the lives of the book's readers; the work has had muted significance
and has perhaps even misled earlier generations.

Both extremes miss an important point: the visions of Revelation carry a universal import. This can be seen by applying to the book the kind of literary analysis I've been using—that is, by reading its text to infer a pattern that sheds light on contemporary experience. The pattern may be broad enough to encompass the particular concerns of both historicists and futurists while at the same time elucidating the lives of readers from many generations.

One such pattern involves the notion of ending. Though we don't often think about it, our lives are filled with conclusions, long before our death. Some are innocent: a college graduation, a move away from home, a marriage that causes us to leave our parental family as we start a new one. Others are somber: a divorce, the death of a loved one, perhaps even, in the late twentieth century, the possibility of nuclear holocaust. One thing I've derived from reading Revelation as literature is a series of insights about such endings, insights adding up to what we can call—in words borrowed from the critic Frank Kermode—"the sense of an ending." I'd like to examine seven such insights, testing along the way their implications for two very different kinds of endings: graduation and nuclear devastation.

One of the first things I notice when reading Revelation in this light is that the ending it describes is not just a capstone or stopping point, but a kind of fulfillment, a completion of what has gone before. This is implicit in frequent references to God's revealing "what must soon take place" (for example, 1:1 or 10:7) and in comments about those whose names have or have not been "written in the book of life from the foundation of the world" (for example, 17:8)—comments that see this ending as a fulfillment of predestined fate. But I think the notion is more pervasive, if more subtle, in Revelation's many allusions to the rest of the Christian Bible, a Bible that it completes and by implication claims to fulfill. So we read of "one like a son of man" (1:13–16) who sounds like a similar figure in Daniel 7:13–14, and go on to find "the tree of life, which is in the paradise of God" (2:7), manna (2:17), David (3:7), the ark of the covenant (11:19), the serpent, here identified as Satan (12:9), the New Testament figure of "a thief in the night" (3:3; compare Matt. 24:42–44 and 1 Thess. 5:2), and the traditional salutation ("Grace to you and peace . . ." [1:4]) and closing

benediction ("The grace of the Lord Jesus be with all . . ." [22:21])
of a Pauline letter. It is as though the book draws together threads
from earlier parts of the Bible, becoming not just a stopping point
but a culmination of what has come before.

Is this idea of fulfillment applicable to other kinds of endings? It
reminds me of graduation as, not just the end of a school career,
but the completion of years of planning, fulfilling requirements,
and working hard. On another level, it suggests a nuclear holocaust
as, not a quirk, but the end result, intended or not, of the stock-
piling of weapons in an arms race. In ways both innocent and somber, it invites a meaningful perspective on endings of different
kinds.

A second insight I derive from reading Revelation is that in an
ending, individuals can get passively caught up in something overwhelming, something beyond their control. John, the narrator/per-
sona of the book, is not an actor but one acted upon, instructed,
guided, even forcibly moved by those higher up (note how he is
caught up "in the Spirit" in 4:1–2, for example). He tends not to
do, but to watch, not to choose, but to be chosen, not to speak,
but to listen in awe. He resembles Dante in the *Inferno*, guided by
Virgil, compelled by fate to encounter an experience that often
overwhelms him. This, too, suggests to me a useful perspective on
other endings. In graduation, do not the graduates become part of
a process involving many who come before, with, and after them?
They do not control the significance of their degree—a significance
determined by the larger quality and reputation of their school.
They are swept up in a movement that they have not so much
chosen as had imposed upon them. The point is clearer, of course,
regarding nuclear holocaust, which may unleash forces over which
none has control, victimizing every individual, including its per-
petrators. Endings tend to overwhelm us.

Which leads to a third point: the ending in Revelation is mysterious, indescribable, ineffable. Many elements suggest this. There
are cryptic symbols at best partially explained, producing an aura
of mystery; so of a strange woman riding a seven-headed beast we
are told, "This calls for a mind with wisdom: the seven heads are
seven mountains on which the woman is seated" (17:9). There are

those pervasive numbers, with mystical qualities for ancients and moderns alike: so we encounter *four* (four horsemen, four angels, four corners of the earth), *seven* (seven churches, seven lamps, seven stars, seven angels, seven trumpets), *twelve* (twelve gates around the New Jerusalem, twelve tribes of Israel, twelve thousand saved from each tribe). There is paradoxical language, transcending logic and common experience as it reaches for the indescribable; so the Lord God says, "I am the Alpha and the Omega" (1:8), the first and the last, the beginning and the end. And there are explicit references to secrets not yet revealed; so John, about to record a message just heard from the sky, is told, "Seal up what the seven thunders have said, and do not write it down" (10:4). Does this notion of the indescribable characterize other endings? Perhaps it's hard to see in graduation, yet I wonder if the idea of moving out of the womb of school, whether to further education or the so-called real world, isn't, for graduates, a not-fully fathomable experience. In any case, the concept clearly describes nuclear devastation, whose unimaginableness is to me one of its most frightening aspects. Again, this sense of an ending is a quality not just of a book, but of experience too.

A fourth characteristic of ending in Revelation is the ambivalence of the response it elicits, a response marked simultaneously by apprehension and anticipation, fear and desire. I find this quality in the book's descriptive imagery. On the one hand, much of that imagery is fearful, depicting violent, cataclysmic events (the seven plagues of 15:1ff.), or grotesque, distorted, threatening creatures (the locusts of 9:7–11). Yet on the other, much of it is exotic and sensuous, appealing in its luxurious, dazzling richness (the New Jerusalem of 21:18–21). And some imagery paradoxically combines both qualities; so in chapter 8 the appeal of this description—"And another angel came and stood at the altar with a golden censer; and he was given much incense to mingle with the prayers of all the saints upon the golden altar before the throne; and the smoke of the incense rose with the prayers of the saints from the hand of the angel before God"—is quickly balanced by the threat of the next verse—"Then the angel took the censer and filled it with fire from the altar and threw it on the earth; and there were peals of thunder, voices, flashes of lightning, and an earthquake" (vv. 3–5). In short, descriptions in Revelation suggest to me things to be feared and things to be desired, often at the same time. And they remind me of the ambivalence surrounding most endings. Graduates fear leaving the security of school even as they are eager to be through. And the great anxiety produced by even thoughts of nuclear holocaust are accompanied, I suspect, by a perverse fascination of the type that draws many to horror films. Endings rarely produce unmixed responses.

Point five in this developing sense of an ending is a simple observation whose significance is easily overlooked. The ending in Revelation is both caused and characterized by conflict. There are battles on earth, such as those following the opening of the second seal of the great scroll, after which John reports, "And out came another horse, bright red; its rider was permitted to take peace from the earth, so that men should slay one another; and he was given a great sword" (6:4). There are battles in heaven, such as that pitting Michael and his angels against the dragon and his angels (12:7ff.). And there is the final cosmic clash at Armageddon in which the forces of evil, both human and demonic, are finally overcome by the forces of good (19:17ff.). (On a subtler level, I think these conflicts are reinforced by the presentation of the dragon, beast, and second beast—later called the false prophet—of chapter 13 as a perverted parody of their opponents, the God, Lamb, and Spirit who comprise the Trinity.) Again, are not many endings marked by such struggle? Graduation only follows years of "battle" pitting students against requirements, exams, grades, teachers, and each other. More clearly and less figuratively, nuclear holocaust is likely to both result from and be marked by conflict. Endings are seldom free from strife.

Which leads to point six: the ending in Revelation is characterized by retributive justice, by a final accounting based on behavior. This is an intriguing point, for it sets up a twofold tension: first within the book, as the notion of judging deeds rubs against the strain of predestination (again, see 17:8), and then within the New Testament as a whole, as Revelation's concern for justice confronts other books' emphasis on mercy. Nonetheless, the drum of justice—and concomitant justifiable anger—is continually sounded here: people of all ranks flee the wrath of the Lamb (6:15–17), the twenty-four elders sing of "the time for the dead to be judged, / for rewarding thy servants . . . , / and for destroying the destroyers of the earth" (11:18), an angel praises the justice of divine judgment (16:5–7), the book of life is opened and the dead are judged "by what they had done" (20:12–13). Throughout we are told of rewards for the faithful and righteous, punishments for the damned—retributive justice in its simplest form. And this raises interesting questions. Is an ending like graduation infused with justice? Perhaps there is in it a final accounting, a reward for those who have succeeded at their tasks, a punishment (no diploma) for the rest. More intriguing, is nuclear devastation likely to be an act of justice? Perhaps its justice will lie not in vindicating the victor and eradicating the enemy, but in its final retribution on the race daring to perpetrate it in the first place.

Finally, point seven: paradoxically, the ending in Revelation is not final; it is a transition to a new order, a prelude to a new beginning. People don't cease to exist at the end of this book; they begin either an eternal reign (22:5) or an eternal damnation (20:15; cf. v. 10). Nor does the world simply disappear, for John tells us at the beginning of chapter 21: "Then I saw a new heaven and a new earth. . . . And I saw the holy city, new Jerusalem, coming down out of heaven from God . . ." (vv. 1–2). Creation is not annihilated, nor does it return to the watery chaos of pre-creation (compare Gen. 1:1–2)—indeed, that chaos is now gone, since "the sea was no more" (21:1b). As is typical of apocalyptic literature, the old order is replaced by a new and different one. Again, Revelation encourages an intriguing perspective on other endings, this time one implicit in the formal name for graduation exercises: commencement. To commence is to begin, not end, and graduation can be seen as the beginning of something new, a transition to a different phase of life. What about a holocaust? It seems to me likely a transition to a new order, but who can say of what kind? Here Revelation leaves me with something to ponder. Endings may be new beginnings, but—witness the different fates of blessed and damned in this book—whether these beginnings bode well or ill may depend on how we are judged "by what we have done."

The Book of Revelation continues to attract and mystify readers of each generation. Attempts to decode it detail by detail—in relation to ancient history, the end of the world, or anything between—have always struck me as fruitless. I agree with critic Kenneth Gros Louis that one of the book's points is "some things in the universe are inexpressible and will remain inexpressible." But mixed with the dazzle and wonder I find striking insights about endings of many kinds. If the book can speak to us of graduation and nuclear devastation, of moving away and losing a loved one, of leaving the parental nest and getting divorced—and ultimately, of course, of meeting our own death—it is a book with implications far-ranging indeed.

Epilogue:
Some Conclusions

With a volume as vast as the Bible, one could go on forever listing conclusions and general observations. Instead, I'll limit myself to six ideas that strike me as pervasive and then invite you to add to, detract from, or modify my list.

What, then, characterizes the literature of the Bible for me?

—*A focus on the concrete, not the abstract.* Instead of a meditation on ethics, we get the *dilemma* of Jephtah; instead of a sermon on interpersonal relationships, we get the *narrative* of Ruth; instead of a treatise on the family, we get the *story* of the Prodigal Son. The world of the Bible is a world of pictures and images.

—*A sense of this world, of things grounded in the here and now.* We encounter the very human activities of David, the "this world" images of the Psalms, the mundane realism of Jesus' parables. For a book often said to be about the hereafter, a good deal of the Bible is firmly rooted in the present.

—*A quest for freedom.* Moses urges Pharaoh to let his people go, Elijah works to liberate Israel from allegiance to foreign gods, Paul struggles for freedom from old rituals and obligations. Perhaps the concept is best summed up in the words of Jesus: "You will know the truth, and the truth will make you free" (John 8:32).

—*A notion of the underdog rising to the top.* So the blinded Samson destroys the Philistines, the boy David emerges from obscurity, Jesus—the cornerstone whom the builders rejected (Matt. 21:42)—is raised from the dead. Longshots often fare pretty well in the Bible.

—*A constant struggle with the deity.* From Job's anguished cries, to Ecclesiastes' soul searching, to Paul's crisis on the Damascus road, the people of the Bible live up to the name *Israel:* "he who struggles with God." None ask "Does he exist?"—there are no atheists here—but all ask "Who is this God, and what does he want from me?"

—*A cyclic process of rising, falling, and rising again.* Creation gives way to the Flood, which leads to a new beginning for Noah and his family. The Israelites' favored position in Egypt gives way to enslavement, which leads to redemption. Jesus' life gives way to death, which leads to resurrection. In each case the third stage of the process differs markedly from the first: "rising again" is not a return to the status quo, but a renewal that changes and advances. The Bible does not so much turn back on itself as undulate forward.

Surely you can identify other possibilities as you think about the material we have read. I'll also leave this question for you to ponder: is the Bible best seen as a unity, a single coherent work moving inexorably from creation to apocalypse, or as an anthology, a collection of distinct pieces of work? As is often the case, perhaps a position somewhere in between should be considered.

I hope our study of the Bible has made us more aware of the richness of this material. I am convinced this kind of literary analysis, moving from text to patterns to experience, is a good approach, one that opens up the human dimensions of the book without damaging (indeed, some might say, while enhancing) its spiritual and historical significance. If you agree, our time and effort have been well spent.

Selected Bibliography

Primary Sources: Standard Editions of the Bible in English

(Most contain study aids of various kinds. A reference to a religious tradition in an annotation describes the orientation of the translators or editors and does not limit the edition's readers to members of that tradition.)

Good News Bible: The Bible in Today's English Version. New York: American Bible Society, 1976. A rendering into colloquial American English, in the Protestant tradition.

The Holy Bible: King James Version: A Reference Edition with the Apocrypha. New York: American Bible Society, n.d. The most famous and influential English version of the Bible, produced by British Protestants in 1611. The KJV is available in many editions, with varying amounts of study aids.

The Holy Bible: New International Version. New York: New York Bible Society, 1978. A conservative translation in the evangelical Protestant tradition.

The Jerusalem Bible. Edited by Alexander Jones. Garden City, N. Y.: Doubleday, 1966. A Roman Catholic translation based on a French version, compared with Hebrew and Greek manuscripts.

The New American Bible. Translated by members of the Catholic Biblical Association of America. New York: P. J. Kenedy & Sons, 1970. A Roman Catholic translation based on Hebrew and Greek manuscripts.

New American Standard Bible. Philadelphia: A.J. Holman Co., 1971. An updating, in the conservative Protestant tradition, of the American Standard Version of 1901, which was in turn a "modernization" of the King James Bible.

The New English Bible with the Apocrypha. Edited by Samuel Sandmel, M. Jack Suggs, and Arnold J. Tkacik. Oxford Study Edition. New York: Oxford University Press, 1976. A British Protestant translation in modern idiom, independent of the King James tradition. A free, rather than literal, rendering.

The New Oxford Annotated Bible with the Apocrypha: Revised Standard Version. Edited by Herbert G. May and Bruce Metzger. New York: Oxford University Press, 1977. An American updating of the King

James Version in the liberal Protestant tradition. Tends toward a literal, word-by-word rendering.

Tanakh: A New Translation of the Holy Scriptures According to the Traditional Hebrew Text. Philadelphia: Jewish Publication Society of America, 1985. A modern rendering of the Torah, Prophets, and Writings of the Hebrew Bible by Jewish scholars. Originally published in three volumes between 1963–82.

Secondary Sources: Dictionaries, Bibliographies, and Critical Studies

Bible Dictionaries

Buttrick, George Arthur, ed. *The Interpreter's Dictionary of the Bible: An Illustrated Encyclopedia.* 4 vols. New York: Abingdon Press, 1962. Supplementary vol., 1976. Identifies and explains "all proper names and significant terms and subjects in the Holy Scriptures . . . with attention to archaeological discoveries and researches into the life and faith of ancient times." Maps. David Robertson's entry "The Bible as Literature" (pp. 547–51 in the supplementary volume) defines the field, surveys arguments for and against this approach, summarizes critical stances, and provides a bibliography.

Miller, Madeleine S., and J. Lane Miller, eds. *Harper's Bible Dictionary.* 8th ed. Revised by eminent authorities. New York: Harper & Row, 1973. A one-volume desk dictionary that includes many photographs, line drawings, and maps.

Bibliography

Gottcent, John H. *The Bible as Literature: A Selective Bibliography.* Boston: G.K. Hall & Co., 1979. An annotated bibliography of books and articles useful in pursuing literary analysis of the Bible. Includes editions and translations, general reference works, and scholarly and critical material on the whole Bible, its major components, and individual books.

Critical Studies

(This listing emphasizes work of the past twenty-five years. See "Critical Reception: A Short History of the Literary Study of the Bible" for older items of interest.)

Alter, Robert. *The Art of Biblical Narrative*. New York: Basic Books, 1981. Alter defines and defends a literary approach to the Hebrew Scriptures and presents readings of selected passages (mainly from Genesis and Samuel/Kings) studying such literary techniques as type-scenes, repetition, dialogue, narrative reticence, and characterization.

Auerbach, Erich. *Mimesis: The Representation of Reality in Western Literature*. Translated by Willard R. Trask. Princeton: Princeton University Press, 1953. Two essays in this collection represent older, but still valuable, examples of a New Critical approach to the Bible. In "Odysseus' Scar" (pp. 3–33) Auerbach contrasts the literary styles of Homer and the writers of the Hebrew Bible, focusing on the binding of Isaac (Gen. 22). In "Fortunata" (pp. 24–49) he discusses Mark's account of Peter's denial of Jesus.

Crossan, John Dominic. *The Dark Interval: Towards a Theology of Story*. Niles, Ill.: Argus Communications, 1975. A structuralist analysis of narrative distinguishing various types of story and focusing primarily on the parable as a kind of narrative that subverts the world. Studies the parables of Jesus, but also considers Ruth and Jonah as earlier examples. Bibliography.

Detweiler, Robert, ed. "Derrida and Biblical Studies." *Semeia* 23 (1982). Four essays—one by Derrida himself—on the challenge of deconstruction to traditional biblical scholarship.

Fischer, James A. *How to Read the Bible*. Englewood Cliffs, N.J.: Prentice Hall, 1982. Argues the contemporary need to read the Bible as literature and offers practical suggestions for reading various biblical genres, including narratives, laws, reflective passages, the prophets, and prayers. Bibliography.

Fishbane, Michael. *Text and Texture: Close Readings of Selected Biblical Texts*. New York: Schocken Books, 1979. "The author has been particularly concerned with showing how literary analysis can mediate a new sense of the Bible as a complex of religious teachings." Sections focus on narratives, direct speech (including prayer and sermon forms), and selected motifs such as Creation, Eden, and Exodus. An important literary examination of different genres from the Hebrew Scriptures.

Frye, Northrop. *The Great Code: The Bible and Literature*. New York: Harcourt Brace Jovanovich, 1982. A culmination of Frye's oft-repeated assertion that the Bible provides the mythological framework for Western culture. Given its impact on imaginative literature, the Bible must be an imaginative work itself. The Christian Bible is considered as a unified whole in light of language, myth, metaphor, and typology. The introduction promises a later volume that will comment more specifically on the text of the Bible itself.

Good, Edwin M. *Irony in the Old Testament.* 2d ed. Sheffield, Eng.: Almond Press, 1981. A literary analysis focusing on irony in selected books of the Hebrew Bible. Sandwiched between an introductory chapter and an epilogue are essays on Jonah, Saul, Genesis, Isaiah, Ecclesiastes, and Job. "I am inclined to think that the presence of irony in the Old Testament casts a new light on the theological task of interpretation."

Gros Louis, Kenneth R.R., with James S. Ackerman, and Thayer S. Warshaw. *Literary Interpretations of Biblical Narratives.* 2 vol. Nashville: Abingdon Press. Vol. 1, 1974. Vol. 2, 1982. Collections of essays on literary analysis, most emphasizing a New Critical approach (although in volume 2 some attention is paid to structuralism and pedagogical matters). A wider variety of contributors is represented in the second volume, which is divided into sections on Methodology, Genesis, and Literary Approaches to Selected Biblical Narratives.

Kugel, James L. *The Idea of Biblical Poetry: Parallelism and Its History.* New Haven: Yale University Press, 1981. An attempt to "arrive at some comprehensive notion of biblical parallelism," a stylistic feature usually perceived in biblical poetry, and to trace its history from antiquity to the present. Concludes that distinctions between biblical poetry and prose are often artificial and questions the validity of modern literary readings of the Bible.

Lowry, Shirley Park. *Familiar Mysteries: The Truth in Myth.* New York: Oxford University Press, 1982. An archetypal attempt to define what myth is and what it does. Cites many examples from the Bible, as well as from other mythologies and folklore. Sections include: The Symbolic Language of Myths, The Hero, The Compleat Home and the Monster at the Door, and Conquering Death. Bibliography.

Petersen, Norman R. *Literary Criticism for New Testament Critics.* Guides to Biblical Scholarship, New Testament Series. Philadelphia: Fortress Press, 1978. Argues for a literary analysis of the Bible that will complement the historical-critical approach. Discusses literary problems in the historical-critical paradigm and proposes a literary-critical model for historical criticism. Presents case studies of Mark (story time and plotted time in the narrative) and Luke-Acts (narrative world and real world).

Robertson, David. *The Old Testament and the Literary Critic.* Guides to Biblical Scholarship, Old Testament Series. Philadelphia: Fortress Press, 1977. Essays by a scholar trained in both biblical studies and contemporary literary criticism. An introductory chapter on the nature of a literary study of the Bible is followed by specific treatments of Exodus, Job, Psalm 90, and the Prophets. Bibliography.

Ryken, Leland. *The Literature of the Bible.* Grand Rapids, Mich.: Zondervan Publishing House, 1974. A study of selected literary forms in the Bible by an evangelical Christian and professor of English. "I have written for readers of the Bible who wish to understand and enjoy the literary dimension of the Bible and who wish to fit biblical literature into their experience of literature generally." Illustrations and glossary.

Thompson, Leonard L. *Introducing Biblical Literature: A More Fantastic Country.* Englewood Cliffs, N. J.: Prentice-Hall, 1978. A study of the language of the Bible and of the "fantastic world" biblical words create. Covers both testaments and considers such things as syntax, irony, myth, image, metaphor. Illustrations and bibliography.

Trible, Phyllis. *God and the Rhetoric of Sexuality.* Overtures to Biblical Theology Series. Philadelphia: Fortress Press, 1978. A study of female imagery and motifs in the Bible. Traces implications of the metaphor in Gen. 1:27 in which the image of God is seen as both male and female. Special attention is paid to "the tragedy of disobedience in Genesis 2-3, the poetry of eroticism in the Song of Songs, and the struggles of daily existence in the story of Ruth."

Wilder, Amos N. *Early Christian Rhetoric: The Language of the Gospel.* Cambridge, Mass.: Harvard University Press, 1971. The introduction surveys the history of the Bible as literature and defends a modern posture that sees literary and theological approaches intertwined. Chapters focus on New Testament language in terms of modes and genres, dialogue, story, parable, poem, image, symbol, and myth.

Index

The following listing includes books of the Bible (titles capitalized), major issues, and biblical figures to whom more than passing reference is made.

Aaron, 14, 16–17
Absalom, 43–44
ACTS OF THE APOSTLES, 13, *101–108*
Ahab, 47–54
apocalyptic literature, 109, 114
approaches to the Bible
  historical approach, 3–4
  literary approach, 4–10
  spiritual approach, 3
archetype, 101–108

Bathsheba, 42–45
birthing process, 101–108
Boaz. *See* RUTH

Christianity, emergence of, 101–108
CHRONICLES, 53

DANIEL, 110
David, 12, 32–34, 36, *38–46*, 48, 53, 110, 116
DEUTERONOMY, 11, 19, 74–75
devil, 53, 67
disillusionment, 82–88

ECCLESIASTES, *82–88*, 117
Elijah, 15, *47–54*, 56, 57, 116
ending, sense of, 109–115
ethics, 91–95
EXODUS, *11–17*, 19, 23, 53, 58
EZEKIEL, 81

faith, 60–65
Flood, *3–10*, 47–54, 117

GENESIS, *3–10*, 16, 18, 21, 53, 58, 96, 114

God (as subject), 5–9, 47–54, 117
Good Samaritan, *91–95*, 98, 100

hero, 11–17, 26–30
  prejudicial thinking about, 56–58
  tragic hero, 31–37

interpersonal relationships, 74–81

jealousy, 96–100
Jephtah, *18–25*, 116
Jesus, 12, 13, 15, 16, 91–94, 96, 102, 104, 105, 116, 117
JOB, 53, *66–73*, 117
JOHN (GOSPEL OF), 116
John (narrator of REVELATION), 111–14
JONAH, *55–59*
JUDGES, 14, *18–30*, 67
justice, 6–7, 49–50, 96–100, 113–14

KINGS, 15, 45–46, *47–54*
Kushner, Rabbi Harold: *When Bad Things Happen to Good People*, 69

Leeming, David: *Mythology: The Voyage of the Hero*, 12
LEVITICUS, 19, 74, 78
LUKE, 12, *91–100*, 104, 105

MARK, 16
MATTHEW, 12, 13, 110, 116
moral dilemma, 18–25
Moses, *11–17*, 51, 53, 116

Naomi. *See* RUTH
"next-of-kin, the." *See* RUTH
Noah, *5–7*, 16, 117
NUMBERS, 16, 51

Orpah. *See* RUTH

parables, *91–100*, 116
Paul (Saul), 13, *102–107*, 110, 111, 116, 117
personality, philosophical, 82–88
Peter, 104–108
poetry, method for reading, 61–65
politics, 38–46
Prodigal Son, *96–100*, 116
PSALMS, *60–65*, 116

REVELATION, 109–115
RUTH, *74–81*, 116

Samson, 14, *26–30*, 116
SAMUEL, 12, *31–45*, 51, 53
Samuel (the man), 33–39
Satan, 53, 67, 68, 70, 110
satire, 56–59
Saul, *31–37*, 38–42, 51, 53; *See also* Paul
Stephen, 104–106
suffering, problem of, 66–73

theodicy, problem of. *See* suffering
THESSALONIANS, 110
thinking, problems with, 55–59
tragedy. *See* hero, tragic

About the Author

John H. Gottcent holds the Ph.D. in literature from the University of Wisconsin. Since 1970 he has taught at the University of Southern Indiana, where he is professor of English. Among his regular offerings are two courses on literary analysis of the Bible.

Professor Gottcent has studied biblical Hebrew and Greek, participated in Indiana University's Summer Institute on Teaching the Bible in Literature Courses, and served as a member of a year-long series of biblical seminars at the same campus. He also spent a year as visiting research associate at Indiana University, studying biblical scholarship and beginning work on the present volume.

His journal articles include "The Case Against the King James Bible," "Teaching the Bible as Literature: How Valid?," and "The Bible as Literature: A New Way of Teaching Scripture"; he is also the author of *The Bible as Literature: A Selective Bibliography* (Boston: G.K. Hall & Co., 1979). He has contributed two entries to the forthcoming *Dictionary of Biblical Tradition in English Literature* and has spoken frequently on the Bible to professional associations, civic groups, and area churches.